TOM LUTTRELL

Get Ready There Will Be A Storm

60 Game-Changing Business Strategies To Ensure You Thrive In Any Financial Climate

Published in London by **Tom-Capital Publishing**

Editing, Proofreading, and Interior/Layout Design by **ThoroughProof Services**

Acknowledgements

A big thanks to some amazing people in my life for their love and support.

Mum and Dad.

My inspirational son Oliver and gorgeous daughter Bella.

My amazing Brothers and Sisters, John, Anne, Clare, Gary, Lynne and Dave.

My wonderful clients.

Throughout my life and career, there have been so many influential people who have helped me shape my journey.

I was lucky enough very early on in my career to meet some incredible man-managers and motivators in Bob Patmore and Iain Alexander. Both had their different styles and both were the best even to this day I have had the pleasure of working with and learning from. I'm incredibly grateful to have met them. I think about their teachings most days for one reason or another. Bob in particular brings a smile to my face often, especially when I'm dealing with a client issue. He just has a way with words that makes what could be perceived as a complicated or challenging problem real simple.

The journey that I went on with David Garofalo and Stuart McGreevy (detailed in this book) was astonishing and taught me how to believe that really big things happen if you have the timing, team, and plan and you get the execution spot on. Both were visionaries at the time.

The Silver foxes, David Tuson and Tony Granger, laid the foundation for me on how to create and protect wealth for business owners, and both taught me how to raise money from investors and institutions.

My incredible family, who have always been there for me through great times and some of the challenges; all have been amazing at different times.

My partner Jo has been a rock and has put up with me working very early mornings and late nights writing this book and creating my course, Capital Catalyst.

And finally, Tracey Currel for contributing to this book, the Amazing Anil Gupta for his love and guidance, Glenn and Nitesh for driving Tom-Capital and Andrew Smith who has been a great creative entrepreneurial partner.

I know I have missed people out and I'm sorry about this. Love to all.

About the Author

With over 30 years of experience coaching business owners on strategy, raising capital, and scaling, Tom Luttrell is an authority in helping entrepreneurs turn ambition into achievement.

A former corporate financial adviser, global property developer, and sought-after public speaker, Tom has built an impressive track record of success across multiple industries, establishing himself as a leading authority in business growth and investment.

Tom's journey began in the world of corporate advisory, where he advised business owners on wealth creation and protection strategies. His strategic acumen led him to become a stakeholder and director in what became the UK's largest independent financial advisory firm. The firm grew from a team of just 4 into a powerhouse with 81 offices around the world, 2,300 employees, and a peak valuation of over £225 million (approximately £500 million today). What started as a bold idea evolved into a global enterprise through strategic planning, teamwork, innovation, and an unwavering commitment to excellence.

In his second career, Tom co-founded an overseas property development company that achieved remarkable success on four continents. With land holdings exceeding $400 million and projects boasting a Gross Development Value of more than $1.6 billion, Tom's expertise in strategic partnerships, high-impact marketing, and assembling world-class teams positioned the company at the forefront of the industry. His ability to create compelling investment opportunities consistently attracted investors, media attention, and premium real estate ventures.

Beyond his corporate achievements, Tom has taken the stage at some of the most prestigious business and financial events worldwide. He shared the UK platform with Tony Robbins at Tony's Financial Mastery event in Hawaii, part of a team led by David and Stuart helping translate US financial products into their UK equivalent. He was also invited to present his property development investment strategies at the legendary Waldorf Astoria in New York, addressing the largest US pension funds, which collectively represented $3 trillion in investments.

Now, in his third career, Tom is dedicated to helping entrepreneurs bring their visions to life. His proven strategies have enabled businesses and property entrepreneurs to raise millions in funding while optimising operations, leadership, marketing, sales, and team development. Whether guiding start-ups or established enterprises, Tom empowers entrepreneurs to build businesses that thrive in any economic climate.

Recognising the critical need for a structured approach to securing investment, he created **Capital Catalyst: Mastering the Art of Fundraising for Founders,** the only online course that provides a step-by-step roadmap to help entrepreneurs successfully prepare for and attract investors with confidence.

Tom's journey is a testament to the power of vision, resilience, and strategic thinking. Whether you're an experienced entrepreneur or just starting out, his insights and expertise will inspire you to think bigger, work smarter, and achieve extraordinary success.

My Story So Far

In 2008, I thought I had the world at my feet. I was in Bangkok, dining at an amazing restaurant with my business partner. Joining us were two of our English partners who lived in Thailand and the Vice Chairman of Lehman Brothers (Asia).

For those unfamiliar, Lehman Brothers was, at that time, one of the oldest and most successful private investment banks in the world (founded in the US in 1850).

We had just concluded a deal to acquire a large tract of land—about 110 acres. The plan was ambitious: to build a six-star resort. Everything was falling into place—financing, a world-renowned hotel chain, Thailand's most famous tennis coach and his celebrity TV star wife, sports ambassadors, political backing, and more. It was a dream project.

As CEO, I instructed our Thai lawyer, Nettipong, to transfer a non-refundable deposit of over $2 million to finalise the deal. Lehman Brothers was providing the remaining funds through a land loan that would later convert into a construction loan. The deposit was paid, the deal was signed, and all that remained was for Lehman to transfer the funds.

At the time, we had four other resort-focused projects on four continents. Our land assets were valued at around $400 million, with a combined Gross Development Value exceeding $1.6bn.

My partner and I had built the business from scratch. We started in 2002 with very little. He brought solid construction experience. He was in the throes of getting planning approval for a $22 million beachfront development of 12 apartments on the west coast of Barbados today called Coral Cove. Planning was not yet granted and the project could fail.

Together, we made a formidable team—he handled construction, while I managed investment, land negotiations, legalities, sales, marketing, and more.

Before this, I had spent 13 years advising business owners on creating and protecting their wealth as a regulated corporate financial adviser. I loved my work and helping people, something that still drives me today.

In a previous chapter of my career, I had the privilege of helping build the UK's largest independent financial advisory business. Working alongside two visionaries, David Garofalo and Stuart McGreevy, they had anticipated changes in the UK financial services industry and stayed ahead of the curve. Six years later, our company had 2,300 people, 81 offices worldwide, and a valuation of £225m (circa £500m today) when we went public on the London AIM.

It was an amazing ride and I learnt so much about growing a business from scratch, scaling, leadership, sales and marketing, branding, firefighting, raising money, building distribution and ultimately listing. The journey taught me so many invaluable lessons. This was all built on the foundation of my extensive training as a corporate financial adviser.

Now, back to Bangkok. That night, the wine flowed, the Vice Chairman of Lehman was as drunk as a skunk, and everyone was buzzing with excitement. After the meeting, my partner and I sat quietly, smiling at what we had achieved. What I haven't mentioned was that Lehman Brothers had also agreed to be our investment partner for all our global sites. It felt like we had truly arrived.

At that point, we were constantly on the move, flying long-haul nearly every week. It was exhausting. That evening, my partner suggested leasing a private jet. At the time, it didn't seem outrageous—our company was thriving. What could possibly go wrong?

A few days later, I couldn't reach the Vice Chairman. I assumed he was still partying—it wasn't unusual for him. Then I received a call from my London team: Lehman Brothers had collapsed. I was stunned. Like most of the world, I couldn't fully grasp the magnitude of what was happening. The global financial system was crumbling, and with it, so was our business. It was a disaster on a scale never seen since the great depression in the 1920s.

By 2011, I was bankrupt. Thirty years of hard work and investment—gone. It was devastating, not just for me, also for our team who were incredible and our investors, who also lost money.

I didn't see the storm coming. I thought we were unstoppable, **bombproof**. I learnt the hard way that no one is immune to a financial storm.

You see storms come in many shapes, and levels of destructive power. Some are financial and out of your control like the 2008 crash, some are financial and in your control, some are personal, some economic. All of these can come at anytime and some will. As I say, many shapes and sizes, and some can be devastating.

My goal with this book is to share lessons that you can adapt to your own journey. Why now? Two reasons: First, I believe my experiences—good, bad, and everything in between—can truly make a difference. Second, if even one idea in this book sparks a breakthrough for you, my mission is accomplished. And if you take away two or more, I consider that a bonus!

This book is the culmination of over 30 years of business experience across three remarkable careers—each filled with incredible highs, tough challenges, and invaluable lessons. Inside, you'll find **60 real-world, practical strategies** that I've learnt first-hand. Many of these strategies and ideas come with real-life stories that bring them to life, showing you what works, what doesn't, and how to navigate the unpredictable world of business with confidence.

But this isn't just a book—it's a **blueprint for action**. Throughout these pages, I've set you challenges designed to push you beyond your comfort zone and into the realm of real progress. **I encourage you to take them on.** Commit, apply what you learn, and watch the transformation begin.

Also, I am launching three new ventures that perfectly align with the strategies in this book:

1. **Capital Catalyst: Mastering the Art of Fundraising for Founders**

An online course designed to empower entrepreneurs to master the art of fundraising. Twelve (12) Modules packed with insider knowledge, guidance and strategies. **My guarantee is to get founders ready to start approaching investors in just 30 days.** It's a roadmap to investors and money.

More than just a course about fundraising.

Capital Catalyst is supported by a community of like-minded founders, industry professionals, investors, and successful entrepreneurs. Together, we address real-world growth challenges, offering guidance, insights, and support to help business owners navigate the complexities of scaling their businesses.

2. Your deckDNA

This is a specialised service dedicated to helping business owners craft investment decks that captivate and compel. With *Your deckDNA*, business owners develop presentations that stand out, telling their business story in a way that grabs investors' attention and inspires confidence.

3. Tom-Coaching

This is my personalised coaching service tailored specifically for business owners. Through *Tom-Coaching,* I share decades of experience to help entrepreneurs overcome challenges, seize opportunities, and achieve their business goals with clarity and confidence.

For more information about any of these services please visit tom-capital.co.uk

Table of Contents

Acknowledgements.. iii
About the Author..vii
Table of Contents xix
Introduction.. 23
Strategy 1: Never Overleverage..................................... 27
Strategy 2: Make Yourself Financially Independent from your Business.. 37
Strategy 3: Create an Amazing Billboard Before You Raise Money.. 45
Strategy 4: Fearless Hiring Leads to Fearless Growth..... 57
Strategy 5: If You Get Bitten by a Snake, You Have Two Choices; Chase the Snake or Cut Out the Poison..............65
Strategy 6: Make Your Team Members Feel Like Giants 71
Strategy 7: Committee Management Does Not Work.... 79

Strategy 8: Kill Monsters When They Are Small.............85
Strategy 9: Sometimes You Cannot Expect the Unexpected.............91
Strategy 10: The Speed of the Pack is Determined by the Leader.............99
Strategy 11: Reward & Recognition: The Simple Secret to Lasting Success.............107
Strategy 12: A Ship is Safe in the Harbour, but That's Not What Ships Were Built For.............115
Strategy 13: Keep Pumping the Pump.............121
Strategy 14: Pay Your Suppliers Early-Raving Fans......125
Strategy 15: Buying a Company? Cut Off the Head of the Snake.............129
Strategy 16: Politicians, Kings & Princesses.............135
Strategy 17: Derry, the Throat-Cut Sign, and Antonio, the Baby-Faced Assassin.............141
Strategy 18: Walking in the Shadows of Giants.............147
Strategy 19: Good Housekeeping, Not Distrust. Get Everything in Writing.............151
Strategy 20: Belt and Braces—Prepare for Illness and Unexpected Events.............157
Strategy 21: Turn Your Business into a McDonald's—Systemise for Success.............165
Strategy 22: Chet Holmes the Legend: How to Manage Multiple Businesses and Personalities at the Same Time. 173
Strategy 23: Why Do Robbers Rob Banks? Because That's Where the Money Is.............179
Strategy 24: Financial Audit: Cut Costs, Boost Value, and Strengthen Your Business.............185

Strategy 25: Databases/CRM: Building the Foundation for Business Growth and Efficiency.................................193
Strategy 26: You Are Going To Need A Bigger Boat-Raising Money from Investors......................................201
Strategy 27: Always Have Two Business Banks............207
Strategy 28: Seek Out Professionals Who Get You and Care..211
Strategy 29: Train Your Sales Team as If Your Life Depended on It 217
Strategy 30: Polar Explorer Robert Swan and the Russian. 225
Strategy 31: Daily Habits - The Foundation Stone of Success...229
Strategy 32: Never Trust A Wolf in Sheep's Clothing... 237
Strategy 33: The Power of High-Performance Teams with a Common Goal.. 253
Strategy 34: The Dark Days.. 267
Strategy 35: Add Trevor to Your Bowling Team........... 271
Strategy 36: Cybersecurity and Hackers: The Invisible Enemy Why Cybersecurity is No Longer Optional....... 275
Strategy 37: The Numbers Don't Lie—Many Property Development Deals Don't Add Up............................... 283
Strategy 38: Induction Day—Make Day One Amazing. 287
Strategy 39: Email Marketing: Play the Long Game...... 293
Strategy 40: Focus on What You Do Best, Leave the Rest 299
Strategy 41: Know Your Story.. 307
Strategy 42: Your Secret Wealth—Contacts and Connections.. 311

Strategy 43: People's Most Dreaded Fear—Public Speaking....317
Strategy 44: Your Secret Weapon—A Friendly Journalist....325
Strategy 45: Balance....331
Strategy 46: Burnout and Mental Health....337
Strategy 47: AI: You Can't Ignore It....345
Strategy 48: Urgency Fuels Action, Vision Shapes Destiny. 351
Strategy 49: Failure Can Be a Gift....355
Strategy 50: If You're Going to Go Big, Get Fit....361
Strategy 51: The Power of Knowledge....365
Strategy 52: Don't let your Mouth Write a Cheque your Brain Can't Cash - Ben....371
Strategy 53: Your Subconscious Mind and Your Mastermind Group....375
Strategy 54: Tim and Christmas Eve - Never Give Up When You're Raising Money....381
Strategy 55: Know Your Numbers or Die....387
Strategy 56: Keep Your Business Partner Real Close....393
Strategy 57: Networking and Empowering Your Team....399
Strategy 58: Seek Out the Best Financial Advisers....407
Strategy 59: Real Bullets....413
Strategy 60: Golden Nuggets and Hidden Gems-Acquiring Businesses....417
Conclusion....427
A Personal Thank You....431
Smile Train....433
Appendix....435

Introduction

The title of this book says it all: **Get Ready, There Will be a Storm.**

And I can guarantee it.

If you've been in business long enough, you'll know that success isn't about smooth sailing—it's about how well you navigate **the inevitable storms**. Some storms will shake you; others will push you to your limits. But the true test? It's whether you stand firm, adapt, and come out stronger.

Looking back on my own journey, I always felt in control. Sure, there were challenges—setbacks, tough decisions, moments of doubt—but they were manageable, more like passing bad weather than true crises.

Then came **2008.** The global financial crisis didn't just test my resilience—it shattered the foundation I had spent decades building. Overnight, deals vanished, businesses crumbled, investors lost money and once-reliable institutions collapsed. My sturdy, well-built oak table of success suddenly had its legs kicked out from under it.

But here's what I learnt: **the storm doesn't destroy those who are prepared. Most, including my organisation were not.**

I wrote this book not just to help you weather financial storms, but to emerge stronger, more resilient, and ready to thrive. Inside, you'll find battle-tested strategies designed to fortify your business, sharpen your decision-making, create wealth and ensure you're always prepared—no matter what the economy throws your way.

But this book is about more than just business. It's about impact. Through this book I will be supporting the charity Smile Train. The charity provides cleft lip and palate surgeries for children in some of the world's poorest regions—kids who, without this help, would face a lifetime of hardship and ridicule. (More details at the back of the book or visit www.smiletrain.org).

All I ask is this: if this book helps or inspires you, take action. Implement what you learn in your business—and pay it forward whenever you can. Please also support the charity if you can.

Finally, I'd love to hear from you. If these strategies make a difference, let me know. Email me, reach out, and share your story. My contact details are at the back of the book.

Stay strong. Stay ready. The storm is coming—let's make sure you're built to thrive.

Enjoy.

Tom.

Strategy **01**

Never Overleverage

"If you're smart, you don't need leverage. If you're dumb, you shouldn't be using it." - Warren Buffett

What you can't see... can sink you

Overleveraging is the most dangerous financial mistake you can make in my opinion. The problem is simple yet **catastrophic;** you can't see the storm around the corner. Never borrow so much that a single unexpected event could wipe you out. Never.

I learnt this lesson the hard way. When things are going well, it's easy to get caught up in the excitement and take on more debt than you should. But bad times have a way of showing up, often out of your control, and they can hit you hard.

I've experienced **four recessions** and the COVID-19 pandemic. Each one was different, but the lessons they taught me were the same.

Let's take a closer look at 3 of these:

The 1989/90 Recession

I had just entered the financial services industry—talk about bad timing. Mortgage interest rates were at a **staggering 15%**, and anyone who had borrowed too much was in serious trouble. Repossessions hit an all-time high, investments plummeted, and the average homeowner struggled to make ends meet. It was a brutal time for many.

The 2008 Global Financial Crisis

Now this was a **perfect storm of financial devastation.** We all know the reasons it happened, but the consequences were staggering. Some of the world's largest property developers collapsed because they were overleveraged. UK bank Barclays avoided a UK government bailout by raising emergency capital from Middle Eastern investors, including significant contributions from Qatar Holding and the Abu Dhabi royal family. Most countries teetered on the brink of bankruptcy and had to be bailed out.

Businesses in all sectors that had been thriving for decades went under almost overnight. It was a monster recession that only a handful of people predicted.

While exact figures vary, here are some of the key estimated costs:

1. **Overall Global Economic Impact**

$10 trillion - Estimated loss in global GDP from 2008 to 2010 due to the recession.

$19.2 trillion - Estimated loss of global wealth during the financial crisis, including stock market declines, property devaluation, and lost business revenue.

30 million+ jobs lost worldwide due to business closures, layoffs, and slowed economic activity.

2. **Direct Cost to Governments (Bailouts & Stimulus)**

Governments worldwide spent massive amounts bailing out financial institutions and stabilising markets:

USA: $700 billion (TARP - Troubled Asset Relief Program) plus trillions more in Federal Reserve interventions.

UK: £137 billion (government bailouts for banks like RBS and Lloyds).

Eurozone: €1.6 trillion in bank rescue funds across Europe.

China: $586 billion stimulus to counteract the economic downturn.

3. **Business & Stock Market Losses**

$34 trillion - Estimated stock market losses worldwide during the height of the crisis.

50%+ market drop - The S&P 500, FTSE 100, and other major indexes lost over half their value at their lowest points.

Corporate bankruptcies - Major firms

collapsed, including Lehman Brothers ($600B in debt), Washington Mutual ($300B), and AIG ($182B bailout).

Housing market collapse - More than 10 million homes were foreclosed in the U.S. alone.

The total estimated global cost of the 2008 crisis, including bailouts, GDP loss, and wealth destruction, is often cited between $10 trillion and $50 trillion.

COVID-19

Who saw this coming in time to prepare? The pandemic didn't just hurt businesses—it decimated them. Take my barber, for instance, a hardworking Italian man who owned seven shops and employed 28 people. After 37 years of running a successful business, he was left with one shop, £250,000 in debt, and no choice but to return to cutting hair himself. Somehow, he's still smiling, but his story is a stark reminder of how quickly fortunes can change.

The truth is, bad things happen—and often without warning. It doesn't have to be a recession; it could be a sudden shift in your market, an unexpected personal setback, or a global pandemic.

The COVID-19 pandemic had a profound impact on the UK economy, leading to the deepest recession in over three centuries.

Here's an overview of the estimated economic effects:

Gross Domestic Product (GDP): In 2020, the UK's GDP contracted by 9.9%, marking the most significant decline since the Great Frost of 1709.

Government Borrowing and Debt: The Office for Budget Responsibility projected a deficit of £394 billion for the 2020–2021 fiscal year, equivalent to 19% of GDP, representing the highest level of borrowing since World War II.

Unemployment and Workforce Impact: By April 2020, claims for unemployment benefits surged by 856,500, bringing the total to 2.1 million.

The pandemic led to a significant reduction in workforce participation, with over 800,000 individuals exiting the labour market, resulting in an estimated annual loss of £16 billion in tax revenues.

Long-Term Economic Challenges: The rise in long-term sickness has kept 2.8 million people out of work, contributing to decreased productivity and increased welfare costs.

So, here's the lesson: Don't over-leverage yourself to the point where, if the worst happens, you can't recover. Take a close look at your financial position today. Understand your risks and make sure you have a buffer, because when the storm hits – and it will – it's the ones who are prepared that survive and thrive.

Action point: Review all of your lending that's already in place. Review all of your current plans to borrow even more and ask yourself a simple question: can I recover if this goes wrong?

Strategy **02**

Make Yourself Financially Independent from your Business

"It's Not What You Make That Counts—It's What You Keep." -
David Tuson

This invaluable piece of wisdom was shared with me in 1997 by **David Tuson.** In the 90s David was widely recognised as the father of corporate financial planning and one of my early mentors. His training courses and audio packages were legendary.

At the time, I heard it but didn't fully absorb its significance. Looking back, had I truly understood and applied this principle, I would have sidestepped a world of financial pain in 2008.

Today, after decades of experience navigating businesses through economic cycles, I have internalised its power.

Profitability, financial sustainability, and long-term wealth creation are the true measures of success, not just impressive turnover figures.

Let me share three essential financial principles that will help you build a business that not only generates revenue but also **creates lasting wealth and security.**

1. Turnover Is Vanity; Profitability Is Sanity

Many entrepreneurs get caught up in the pursuit of high turnover, believing that bigger numbers equate to business success. But **turnover alone is meaningless if profitability is neglected.**

Cash flow mismanagement is the number one cause of business failure. Without careful financial oversight, even businesses with strong sales can collapse under the weight of excessive costs and poor cash flow planning.

Strategic Financial Planning: Map out how you'll manage revenue growth while ensuring expenses remain controlled.

Robust Cash Flow Management: Secure lines of credit, establish emergency reserves, and create financial buffers to sustain operations in lean periods.

Continuous Monitoring: Regularly review profitability metrics, track expenses meticulously, and adjust business strategies accordingly.

Remember: **You never go bust by making a profit.** Prioritise financial efficiency and sustainability over vanity-driven revenue targets.

"Do not save what is left after spending, but spend what is left after saving." - Warren Buffett

2. Build Wealth Outside Your Business

A common mistake business owners make is pouring all their resources into their company while failing to secure personal financial independence. **Your business should be a tool for wealth creation, not your sole financial lifeline. This is so profound I will repeat it: Your business should be a tool for wealth creation, not your sole financial lifeline.**

Diversification Is Key: Invest in **income-**

generating assets such as property/ real estate, stocks and shares, or passive income streams that supplement your business earnings. Perhaps your thing is trading currency? Whatever you prefer and understand, just diversify.

Wealth Protection Strategies: Utilise financial vehicles such as **trusts, tax-efficient investment portfolios, and pension funds** to build long-term security.

Exit Strategy Planning: Develop a personal financial roadmap that ensures you're financially secure whether you stay in business or exit.

Review Strategy 20 to protect your assets if disaster strikes.

A business can be a powerful engine for wealth, but **true financial freedom comes from diversified assets** that work for you outside your primary enterprise.

3. Don't Put All Your Eggs in One Basket

Many entrepreneurs assume that selling their business will be their golden retirement plan. However, banking **100% on your company's future sales** is a **risky gamble, in fact, I would call it a mistake.**

Market Uncertainty: Economic downturns, industry disruptions, and unexpected crises can significantly impact your business valuation.

Buyer Dependence: Mergers and acquisitions don't always materialise as planned. Potential buyers back out, and deals fall apart.

Liquidity Planning: Ensure that you are not solely reliant on a future sale by **building liquid assets** that give you financial security at any stage of your business journey.

By creating multiple **income streams and exit options**, you mitigate risk and protect your financial future from unpredictability. In short, you become STORMPROOF.

Key Takeaways

Profitability over Turnover: Revenue means nothing without healthy profit margins and effective cash flow management.

Financial Independence: Build assets and investments outside your business to create long-term wealth.

Risk Mitigation: Don't rely solely on your business sale for financial security—develop multiple safety nets.

Plan for the Long Game: Financial sustainability comes from making **strategic wealth-building decisions** over time, not chasing short-term gains.

David's advice rings as true today as it did in 1997: **It's not what you make that counts—it's**

what you keep. Master this principle, and you will build a business—and a financial future—that is both prosperous and resilient.

Action Point: Construct a personal financial strategy that includes wealth-building investments **outside your business.** Start today by reviewing your current portfolio, identifying gaps, and implementing steps toward long-term security.

Include property investments in your plan. I have always believed in bricks and mortar. Remember strategy 1, don't over-leverage.

By embedding these strategic financial principles into your mindset, you're not just building a profitable business—you're securing **lasting financial freedom.**

Strategy 03

Create an Amazing Billboard Before You Raise Money

"A good reputation is more valuable than money." - Publilius Syrus (Roman philosopher)

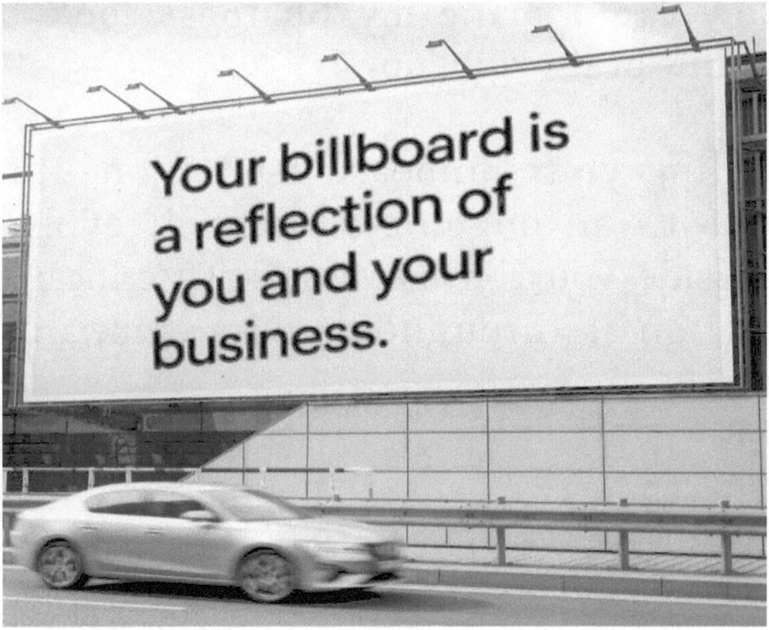

What's a Billboard, you ask? Your Billboard is the ultimate reflection of you and your business—who you are, what you stand for, your people, your products, and your company's story. It's not just your business plan or your investment deck; it's an amalgamation of everything that represents you.

Your Billboard should answer one key question:

"How can I make my business look its absolute best—right now?

Building your Billboard isn't a one-time task—it's an ongoing process. It evolves alongside your business, and it's critical to work on it throughout your company's lifecycle.

Let me share two game-changing examples to illustrate its power:

1. In 2005 my property development company was starting to take off. I was very proud of how well it was going even though it was bloody tough, start-ups always are. Even though we were going great I intuitively knew that to break through to the next level I had to make a big change – change gear. The problem was we were so busy it was difficult to take time out and think. Fortunately, I had learnt many years before that what works best for me is to take quality time out to think.

With the word Billboard ringing in my ears, that is what I did. I was fortunate enough to be overseas and next to a beach. My thought process was simple and that was what can we do today to make a massive difference to our business? I was manifesting. The answer did not come for 2 days, but when it did it was seismic – game-changing.

I spoke with my business partner and told him that what we needed was someone with a significant track record in property, someone with grey hair (quite ironic as my business partner was bald)! He came around to my way of thinking eventually but to be fair he had his reservations, mostly because at that time all decisions were normally made between the two of us and he didn't want to lose any day-to-day control. I advised that we were looking for a non-Exec director who was part-time and he warmed to that.

With everything agreed upon and me manifesting, I set about looking for the right person. It was not easy. I spoke to some people who just did not fit and then one day my non-exec appeared as if by magic at the most unlikely of places. One of my mentors in financial services (Bob) lived in a beautiful home in one of the lovely villages in Buckinghamshire (he still does). I went across to see him one day as he was working with us on another project. He was an investor and shareholder. We were chewing the fat and I happened to mention that I was looking for a heavyweight property guy/woman with a significant track record in property and my friend said, "I think I know the guy, let me have a word with him."

A few days later, I got a call from Bob, he said for me to come around and see him the next day. When I got there, he said that he had spoken to his friend and that we were going around for a chat. I thought going where? We walked to the end of his very long drive, turned left about 50 yards, walked across the road, and walked up another long drive, and that was where I met Trevor for the first time (Trevor was a great man, with an amazing career. He has now passed. Bless him).

Trevor (MBE) was in his late 70s and he had grey hair! His resume was beyond my wildest dreams.

Now imagine this, Trevor had run Hong Kong Land which at the time was the largest property company in the world! I had to pinch myself, was this really happening?

About 2 weeks later, Trevor joined the board and that was when our company took off faster than I could have imagined. Everyone listened to us, Prime Ministers, Politicians, Royalty, Investors, and land owners. Billboard! Billboard!

The second example followed a similar path only this did not involve one person; it involved 4. I was working on our sales strategy for a large 1200-acre site we had in Spain. I was thinking about how we could attract buyers of homes to us in a very competitive market at the time. Our site was wonderful, really rural, not too far from the ocean and the site sat at the bottom of a beautiful whitewash Spanish village that sat on top of a hill, perfect. We were given permission to build two 18-hole golf courses and an academy. I recruited a very famous golf course designer called Dave Thomas.

Now Dave was famous for designing many great courses but is most famous for the course at the Belfry in the UK called the Brabazon, which has been the venue for the Ryder Cup over the years (sorry, you non-golfers if that means nothing to you).

Whilst having Dave on board would make a difference to my Billboard, I knew it would not be a sales gamechanger, I needed something new. I decided that we should create a section on the site dedicated to sports. My business partner thought the idea was solid as did the rest of our team. We decided that if we could create an equestrian centre, I would approach Ewan, a great guy, sports agent back in the day, and entrepreneur, to see if we could sponsor Zara Philips and Mike Tindall. Zara, an Olympian horserider and the late Queen's granddaughter, Mike had just won the rugby World Cup with England. It was a moonshot that landed. Off the back of this, I also managed to do the same with Martin Johnson the England rugby World Cup-winning captain. I also managed to do the same with Irish rugby legend Shane Byrne and Martin Johnson the England rugby World Cup-Winning captain…amazing.

Later on, we also managed to persuade Kevin Pietersen to join our stable of ambassadors for one of our Caribbean projects (Kevin was one of the best cricketers of his generation).

When my team and I were ready, we launched our sales strategy. We had planning permission for 1200 homes. Our plan was to sell 300 homes off plan. We achieved our goal in just 8 weeks.

I have many other examples I could share. Whenever I take on a new client who wants to raise money for their company from equity investors I always start with their Billboard.

Building Your Own Billboard: What You Need to Focus On

To raise money, win deals, and grow your business, constantly **refine and expand your Billboard.** Here's what you should be working on:

Marketing Collateral – Your website, branding, pitch decks, and all external materials must reflect **excellence.**

Social Media & Digital Presence – Even if you dislike social media, investors and partners expect to see **a strong online presence.**

Financials & Projections – Your financials should be **clear, professional, and investor-ready.**

Your Investment Deck & Business Plan – These must **clearly communicate** why someone should invest in you.

Your Bio & Team Profile – Investors back **credible, experienced teams.** Ensure your bio and senior leadership team **stand out.**

Board & Advisory Roles – Strengthen your business by bringing in **industry leaders, respected figures, and experienced non-executive directors.**

Press & Media Exposure – Get published, get mentioned, and **get in front of the right audiences.**

Strategic Alliances & Endorsements - Build relationships with **industry influencers and government officials** where relevant.

Client & Partner Testimonials - Your track record should speak for itself through **credible third-party endorsements.**

Key Takeaways

Your Billboard is your business identity – It's what investors, clients, and partners see before they ever meet you. Make it strong.

High-level endorsements & partnerships create trust - Align yourself with industry leaders, strategic partners, and key influencers.

Perception = Credibility. You can be great,

but if no one perceives you as great, it won't matter.

Refinement is constant. Your Billboard is never finished; **keep improving, keep expanding, keep strengthening.**

Action Points: Take quality time away from your business. Turn your phone off for the day, even two, and think. Don't rush this process. Ideas will flow but they may take a few days to show themselves!

Step 1: Audit Your Billboard. Take an honest look at how your business is currently perceived. Identify weak spots.

Step 2: Develop 3 High-Impact Upgrades. Example: Identify three things you can **improve immediately** (e.g., website, board members, investor deck).

Step 3: Secure a Game-Changer. Think strategically: **Who could elevate your**

business overnight? Start **networking, engaging, and making it happen.**

The stronger your Billboard, the more opportunities will come knocking. Build it, refine it, and watch your business transform.

Strategy 04

Fearless Hiring Leads to Fearless Growth

"It doesn't make sense to hire smart people and then tell them what to do; we hire smart people so they can tell us what to do." - Steve Jobs

Always recruit people onto your board or team who are better than you at what they do.

This topic is close to my heart, and for good reason. Throughout my career, I've seen the incredible power of assembling the right team—and the devastating consequences of getting it wrong. Later in this book, I'll talk about Mavericks and Snakes, and the kinds of hires you need to watch out for, but for now, let's focus on why recruiting the best is non-negotiable for building a thriving business.

Why Surround Yourself with Talent?

As a business owner, your goal isn't to be the smartest person in the room—it's to assemble a room full of people whose collective brilliance outshines your own. Talented individuals bring fresh perspectives, solve problems faster, and push your business beyond what you could achieve alone.

Too often, founders let fear or ego hold them back from hiring the best. They worry about being overshadowed or losing control. But here's the truth: **your company's success will depend more on the team you build than on your personal abilities.** If you're the bottleneck, your growth will stall. If you empower others to lead and excel, your business will soar.

Lessons from My Experience

I've been fortunate to be part of two companies that succeeded largely because of the extraordinary people on our teams. At every level, from the boardroom to admin staff, we worked with individuals who were not only exceptional at their jobs but also aligned with our vision and values.

For example, in one of my ventures, I brought on a board member with decades of industry expertise and connections I couldn't dream of accessing on my own. His insights and network opened doors that accelerated our growth exponentially. That decision alone made a huge difference to our bottom line.

The Qualities to Look For

When recruiting the best, focus on more than just their technical skills or impressive CV. The most impactful team members share the following traits:

1. **Alignment with Your Vision**

You can teach skills, but you can't teach passion for your mission. Look for people who genuinely believe in what you're building.

2. **Complementary Skills**

Hire for your blind spots. Identify areas where you lack expertise or bandwidth and bring in specialists who can fill those gaps better than you ever could.

3. **Strong Values and Integrity**

Talent alone isn't enough. You need people you can trust—those who will act in the company's best interest, even when no one is looking.

4. A Growth Mindset

The best hires are those who constantly strive to learn and improve. They challenge themselves—and you—to reach new heights.

Building a Culture of Excellence

Recruiting the best isn't a one-time task; it's an ongoing commitment to excellence. Here are a few strategies to foster this culture:

- **Invest in Recruitment**: Don't settle for the first candidate who seems "good enough." Take your time to find the right fit.

- **Create an Attractive Environment**: Top talent wants to work for a company that values them, provides growth opportunities, and shares their passion.

- **Empower Your Team**: Once you've hired the best, give them the tools, autonomy, and support they need to thrive.

Don't Be Afraid to Shine a Spotlight on Others

As a leader, your job isn't to outshine your team; it's to elevate them. Never be afraid of hiring people who might one day surpass you. Their success reflects your ability to lead effectively.

The Ultimate Goal

The ultimate goal of recruiting the best is to make your business self-sufficient. Imagine stepping away for a month or a year, knowing that your team will not only maintain the business but also grow it. That's the power of surrounding yourself with the right people.

Final Thought

Recruiting the best isn't just about filling roles; it's about future-proofing your business. It's about creating a team that can weather storms, innovate under pressure, and take your vision further than you ever imagined.

So, embrace the challenge. Seek out people who intimidate you with their brilliance, who push you to think bigger and work harder. Trust me—it's one of the most rewarding investments you'll ever make.

Action point: Who could you hire today that would make a massive difference to you and your business? This hire could be an employee on a salary or a board member who would join for performance pay and some ownership in your business.

Strategy 05

If You Get Bitten by a Snake, You Have Two Choices: Chase the Snake or Cut Out the Poison

"When someone shows you who they are, believe them the first time." - Maya Angelou

You've probably heard this saying before in your career. But the real question is: did you *really* hear it? Let's take a moment to unpack it.

In today's fast-paced business environment, you need everyone on your side. Everyone. Unfortunately, humans are unpredictable—some will unintentionally let you down, while others might be manipulative or downright toxic.

Over the past 30+ years, having recruited and trained thousands of people, I've seen just about every type of personality. The hard truth? When someone is toxic—be it a board member or someone in admin—you need to act fast.

The Snake in the Office

Toxic individuals won't change. They never do. Worse, they can infect your team's morale and destabilise your entire operation. These people can drain energy, create mistrust, and shift focus away from growth and success. The sooner you remove them, the better off your company and culture will be.

A Story That Says It All

I love the story of the scorpion and the frog. It's simple but profound. On a hot summer day, a scorpion and a frog are walking along a riverbank. Both were hungry and needed to cross to the other side where there was plenty of food.

The scorpion says to his friend, "You're a great swimmer. Why don't you carry me across on your back?"

The frog hesitates. "But you're a scorpion! If you sting me, we'll both die."

The scorpion reassures him, "That would be ridiculous! Why would I sting you and doom us both? Trust me."

After a moment's thought, the frog agrees, and the scorpion climbs onto his back. Halfway across the river, the frog feels a sharp pain—he's been stung.

"Why would you do that? Now we'll both die!" cries the frog.

The scorpion replies, "I couldn't help myself. I'm a scorpion. It's in my nature."

The Lesson

The moral of the story? Don't let scorpions into your business or life. Their nature will eventually lead to harm, no matter what they promise or how sincere they seem.

Spotting the Snake

Over time, you'll develop a radar for toxic behaviour. Common traits include:

- Manipulation and backstabbing.
- Undermining others to elevate themselves.
- Spreading negativity or gossip.
- Being consistently unreliable or dishonest.
- They always use negative humour in a group environment.

When you spot these behaviours, act swiftly and decisively. Waiting too long only gives the snake more time to spread their poison.

Cutting Out the Poison

Dealing with toxic individuals doesn't mean burning bridges or seeking revenge – it means preserving the health of your business and team. Address the situation professionally, document behaviours if necessary, and move them out of your organisation as quickly as possible. Your team will thank you, and your business will thrive in their absence.

Building a Snake-Free Culture

The best defence against snakes is building a strong, transparent culture where trust, respect, and accountability are prioritised. Encourage open communication, recognise positive contributions, and foster an environment where everyone feels valued.

In the end, every leader faces challenges with difficult individuals. But remember, your responsibility is to protect the greater good of your team and business. Spot the snakes early, and always choose to cut out the poison.

Action point: You already know the answer! Kill monsters when they are small. Deal with anyone who is toxic in your business and life, today! Be gracious but get it done. Follow HR regulations.

Strategy 06

Make Your Team Members Feel Like Giants

"Treat people as if they were what they ought to be, and you help them become what they are capable of being." - Johann Wolfgang von Goethe

One of the greatest skills I learnt from an old mentor was how to make people on my team feel incredible about themselves—how to make them feel like giants.

When people feel good about themselves, they're more likely to perform at their peak. Beyond that, creating an environment where everyone feels valued and capable is the key to building a team that consistently achieves its goals.

Making someone feel like a giant isn't about manipulation—it's about genuinely caring for them and helping them recognise their strengths and potential. It's about uplifting others, encouraging them to stretch beyond their comfort zones, and empowering them to do things they may have doubted they could achieve.

Here are some of the best ways to make someone feel great about themselves:

1. **Acknowledge Their Strengths**
Highlight what they do well, both privately and publicly. Let them know their contributions are noticed and valued.

2. **Give Specific Praise**
Instead of generic compliments, provide detailed feedback like, "Your presentation was fantastic because it was so well-researched and engaging." This shows that you're paying attention.

3. **Encourage Growth**
Believe in their ability to take on bigger challenges. Say things like, "I know you're capable of handling this project—you've got the skills and mindset to succeed."

4. **Listen Attentively**
When someone speaks, give them your full attention. Show that their thoughts, ideas, and concerns matter.

5. **Show Gratitude**
Thank them for their hard work, ideas, or

support. A heartfelt "thank you" can go a long way.

6. **Empower Decision-Making**
Trust them to make decisions in their role. Letting someone take ownership of their work builds their confidence.

7. **Offer Opportunities for Growth**
Whether it's training, a challenging project, or mentorship, give them opportunities to expand their horizons.

8. **Celebrate Their Wins**
Recognise and celebrate achievements, no matter how small. Whether it's a team shoutout or a simple congratulatory email, celebrate their progress.

9. **Show Empathy**
Be understanding of their challenges or setbacks. Let them know it's okay to make mistakes and that you're there to support them.

10. **Be Consistent in Your Support**
Show encouragement consistently, not just when it's convenient or during performance reviews.

11. **Promote Collaboration**
Highlight their role in the team's success and how their efforts positively impact others.

12. **Be Sincere**
Avoid hollow flattery. Genuine acknowledgment has a far greater impact than superficial compliments.

13. **Invest in Their Development**
Provide resources, coaching, or opportunities that help them grow both personally and professionally.

14. **Create a Positive Environment**
Build a culture where people feel safe to express themselves, share ideas, and take risks without fear of judgement.

15. **Believe in Them**
Sometimes, people just need to hear, "I believe in you." Confidence in them from someone they respect can be transformative.

By integrating these practices into your leadership style, you'll create a culture where people feel like giants—strong, capable, and inspired to give their best. When you elevate your team, you elevate your business.

Action Points: Empowering Your Team to Feel Like Giants

Step 1: Create a Recognition & Motivation Plan
Make a list of all your team members and outline specific ways you will **motivate, acknowledge, and reward** them over the next 3 months. Think beyond monetary incentives—personalised recognition, career development opportunities, and meaningful gestures make a lasting impact.

Step 2: Celebrate Wins Publicly & Correct Privately

When a team member excels, **recognise their achievement publicly**—whether it's in a company meeting, email, or social media post. **Corrections and constructive feedback should always be given privately** to maintain trust and morale.

Step 3: Involve Leadership for Larger Teams

If your organisation is large, engage your **senior management team** to ensure recognition and motivation **reach every level of the business.** Make recognition a company-wide culture, not just a top-down initiative.

Step 4: Be Consistent & Intentional

Recognition should not be random—**make it a structured habit.** Whether through weekly shout-outs, monthly awards, or quarterly reviews, ensure employees feel valued **regularly** and not just during performance appraisals.

By lifting your team up and making them feel **like giants**, you cultivate **loyalty, high performance, and a thriving company culture.**

Strategy 07

Committee Management Does Not Work

"A committee is a group that keeps minutes and loses hours." - Milton Berle

This one always makes me smile—mostly because it's such a classic example of learning the hard way. Is this you? If not, remember this story, because it might save you from making the same mistake.

There I was in Mayfair, surrounded by my senior management team. I was around 40 years old, business was booming, and we were breaking records left, right, and centre. My team was exceptional—arguably one of the best senior management teams ever assembled in UK financial services.

They were ambitious, intelligent, hardworking, diverse, and full of energy.

What could possibly go wrong?

Well, apparently, I had a brain transplant. I'd been reading—a habit I recommend but occasionally regret—and stumbled across a book on inclusion in management. I'm sure the author meant well, but that book? Absolutely disastrous.

It was Christmas time, and the team was buzzing with excitement. To add to the moment, I'd invited my mentor Bob to join the meeting—probably because I wanted to show him how far I'd come. Big mistake.

The meeting started as usual, with a full agenda that I read out. But then, for reasons I still don't fully understand, I decided to take a back seat. I announced to the team that I wanted them to lead the discussion, share their thoughts, and collaborate. I thought I was empowering them.

The next three hours? Pure chaos.

These were highly successful, driven individuals, but without a clear leader guiding the discussion, it devolved into a mess of competing opinions, circular arguments, and unresolved conflicts.

When the meeting ended, they all headed to the bar. Bob stayed behind. He turned to me and said words I will never forget: "Tom, **never fucking do that again**. Committee management does not work."

He paused for a moment and added, "The buck always stops with you. Good or bad, it's your responsibility. Remember, the speed of the pack is determined by the leader. There can only be one lead wolf."

It was a tough but invaluable lesson, and I've carried it with me ever since. When it comes to managing high-performance teams, inclusion is vital—absolutely. Listen to your people. Value their input. Adopt the best ideas. But leadership is not a democracy.

At the end of the day, the responsibility is yours. The team looks to you for clarity, direction, and decisions. Don't hand over the reins unless you're prepared to deal with the consequences.

Key Takeaways:

1. **Inclusion Matters, But Leadership Is Essential:** Listen to your team and involve them in discussions, but never abdicate your responsibility as the leader.

2. **Clarity and Direction Are Key:** High-performing teams thrive on clear goals and decisive leadership.

3. **You're the Lead Wolf:** A pack follows its leader. The speed, efficiency, and morale of the team depend on you taking charge.

Your team needs a leader, not a committee. Be the lead wolf.

Action point: This may be advice that seems contrary to the message in this strategy however, if you have a large senior management team you should develop one of them who can stand in your shoes and deliver leadership if you are not around, especially if you get ill or have a bad accident. This person will already be liked and respected by the majority today. Bring them along quietly without too much fuss, don't make it obvious. Perhaps they start to run the Friday morning update meetings or similar tasks. Soon enough everyone will know who is the second in command. Identify this person and have a meeting with them to sound them out.

Strategy 08

Kill Monsters When They Are Small

"Take care of the little things and the big things will take care of themselves." - Richard Carlson

Letting problems linger—whether in your business or personal life—is a recipe for disaster. Trust me on this. Problems rarely resolve themselves and often grow bigger, more complex, and harder to handle. They develop legs, spread, and, before you know it, can take over everything. If you haven't already mastered this skill, start practicing it today.

Some people may resist this approach initially because it's likely a shift in your management style. But believe me, confronting issues head-on and addressing them promptly will save you immeasurable pain, time, and resources in the future.

A Practical Approach

Try this: communicate to everyone in your team that from now on, if a potential problem arises, you will address it quickly, fairly, and privately. Let them know this is a standard operating principle, not a punitive measure.

Once they understand you're serious, the message will sink in.

The key? Stick to your word. Don't shy away from tough conversations, and don't let fear of confrontation delay action.

A Story About Monsters

I'll never forget discovering that someone on my team had been stealing from us. It hit me like a punch to the gut. The shock wasn't just about the theft—it was who it was. This guy wasn't just a colleague; he was a friend. Years earlier, he had even been my boss, someone I deeply respected.

When I first heard the accusation, I didn't want to believe it. But as the evidence became undeniable, I knew I had to act. Letting it slide wasn't an option—not for the sake of my team, my business, or even myself.

I was both angry and nervous as I called the meeting. It wasn't easy, but I approached it with clarity and respect. I told him how much I admired him and acknowledged that I knew he was struggling financially. But I also made it clear that his actions were unacceptable.

The meeting was short. I asked him to gather his things and leave the building immediately. It was painful—more than I expected—but it was the right decision. Ignoring the issue would have sent a message to the rest of the team that I tolerated dishonesty, and that wasn't something I could allow.

Why This Matters

Small problems rarely stay small. A minor issue today can become a full-blown crisis tomorrow if left unchecked. Whether it's a toxic team member, a financial irregularity, or operational inefficiency, tackling issues early protects the integrity of your business and maintains trust within your team.

Key Takeaways

1. **Act Fast:** Address problems as soon as you're aware of them. Don't let them fester.

2. **Be Clear and Fair:** Communicate your actions decisively but with respect. Clarity minimises misunderstanding and sets a strong precedent.

3. **Protect Your Environment:** By dealing with issues swiftly, you create a culture of accountability and professionalism.

Kill monsters while they're small. It's uncomfortable at the moment, but it saves you from dealing with much bigger beasts down the road.

Get Ready, There Will be a Storm

Strategy 09

Sometimes You Cannot Expect the Unexpected

"Everyone has a plan until they get punched in the mouth." - Mike Tyson

Sometimes life throws situations your way that are so bizarre or shocking they leave you speechless. These moments remind us of the limits of preparation—there are things you simply cannot foresee. When running a business, you need to be ready to respond, adapt, and learn from the unexpected.
Here are three real stories from my career that drove this lesson home:

1. The Drunken Recruit

I once had an office in Bracknell where we held weekly recruitment evenings to find the next star in financial services. One cold winter night, only two people showed up. One wasn't a fit, but the other, let's call him Jim, stood out. He was polished, sharp, and oozed potential. Over a month, I met with him three times, and each meeting confirmed my initial instincts—Jim was exceptional.

When Jim said he wanted to join, I was thrilled. He asked for a small advance to get through the initial months, which wasn't unusual for commission-based roles. I agreed and proudly told my senior managers I'd recruited a game-changer.

On Monday morning, Jim was set to start. By 8 a.m., no sign of him. By 10 a.m., my PA walked in, visibly concerned. "Tom, we have a problem," she said. Apparently, Jim was in the men's toilet, drunk, trousers around his ankles, screaming at anyone who walked in!

I found him, helped him out of the building, and on the way out, he asked if he still had a job—and if could I lend him £50!

Lesson learnt: Even your best recruits can let you down. Despite your best efforts, people can surprise you—sometimes in spectacularly disappointing ways. Don't take it personally. Be ready for curveballs.

2. The Levitation Revelation

Another time, I recruited a woman, let's call her Jane. She started strong – sharp, punctual, professional, and generated immediate business.

But after 8 weeks, she began slipping. Concerned, I scheduled a one-on-one, and she shared some personal struggles at home. I offered support, hoping it would help. I really liked her.

That evening, we travelled together to meet a client. On the drive back, in the pouring rain, she opened up more about her family life. Then, out of nowhere, she said her father often scolded her for walking on creaky stairs. I made a light comment, and she replied, "Normally, he doesn't catch me because I levitate over the stairs."

I froze. Levitate? She went on to describe, in great detail, how she could float up and down the stairs to avoid making noise. I was dumbfounded. Not wanting to distract her while driving, I suggested she keep her eyes on the road.

Jane didn't return to work after that, despite my attempts to reach her.

Lesson learnt: Some things defy explanation. Not every situation has a moral or a clear takeaway. Sometimes, you just have to laugh, shake your head, and move on.

3. The Gambler's Mask

Jack (not his real name), a colleague in the financial services industry, had been working for over a decade and was universally liked and trusted. He was professional, articulate, and had great rapport with clients.

One day, an elegant older woman came to see me, visibly upset. She explained that Jack had been handling £175,000 of her late husband's money for nearly a decade, but recently, payments had stopped, and excuses started piling up.

I reassured her, confident Jack would never do anything untoward. But when I investigated, the truth was devastating. Jack had a hidden gambling problem and had spent every penny of her money. He was arrested shortly after, and I never heard from him again. I was so shocked.

Lesson learnt: Always look behind the mask, especially when your team manages people's money or trust. Build strong relationships with your team, look for red flags, and establish systems to prevent these situations. Trust is essential, but blind trust is dangerous.

Key Takeaways

1. **Expect the Unexpected**: Even the best-laid plans can be derailed by unforeseen events. Learn to adapt and act quickly.

2. **Look Beyond the Surface**: People are complex, and appearances can be deceiving. Stay observant and proactive in assessing character and performance.

3. **Separate Emotion from Action**: It's easy to feel betrayed or disillusioned, but emotional reactions won't fix the problem. Stay composed and focused on resolution.

4. **Prepare for Shocks**: Systems, safeguards, and regular reviews can help mitigate risks, but nothing is foolproof. Be ready for surprises and learn to respond with resilience.

Finally, some situations will leave you scratching your head, asking, "How could this happen?" But that's life in business—and the sooner you accept it, the better prepared you'll be to navigate the chaos. Always expect the unexpected.

Get Ready, There Will be a Storm

Strategy 10

The Speed of the Pack is Determined by the Leader

"A leader is one who knows the way, goes the way, and shows the way." - John C. Maxwell

This powerful saying has always resonated with me because it serves as a wake-up call. It encapsulates the essence of leadership: your actions, attitude, and energy set the tone for your entire team. If you want a high-performing team, you must embody the behaviours and values you expect from them.

Lead by Example

Early in my career, I realised that being a leader meant going first. I did the things others avoided, faced challenges head-on, and got comfortable being uncomfortable. This not only earned the respect and loyalty of my team but also set a standard for behaviour. They didn't just follow me—they passed these lessons on to others.

If you want to build a team that thrives, you must be the "lead wolf." Never ask someone to do something you wouldn't do yourself. Whether it's staying late to close a deal, making a difficult phone call, or stepping into a crisis, your willingness to act will inspire your team to do the same.

Your Team is Watching

As a leader, you're always under observation. Your team studies your habits—good and bad—and often mirrors them. If you're punctual, organised, and proactive, they'll take those cues. But if you're disorganised, complacent, or negative, they'll pick up on that too.

What's more? They talk. Your actions and decisions become the subject of conversations when you're not in the room. You may not realise the ripple effect of your behaviour, but it's always there.

Beware of Complacency

The most dangerous time for a leader is when the business is thriving, especially after years of hard work. Success can breed complacency, and complacency is contagious. If you take your foot off the gas, so will your team. Bad habits will seep in, and the culture you worked so hard to build can start to erode.

That's why self-awareness and discipline are critical. As the leader, you set the pace for everyone else. If you maintain high standards, your team will too. If you become sloppy, don't be surprised when performance drops across the board.

Cultivate a Leadership Mindset

To be the leader your team needs, consider these guiding principles:

1. **Embrace Accountability:** The buck stops with you. Whether the outcome is good or bad, own it. Accountability builds trust and respect.

2. **Prioritise Growth:** Constantly push yourself to learn, improve, and evolve. Your team will take their cues from your commitment to growth.

3. **Communicate Clearly:** Share your vision, set expectations, and provide regular feedback. Transparency fosters alignment and minimises confusion.

4. **Foster Positivity:** Your energy influences your team's morale. Stay optimistic and solution-focused, even in challenging times.

5. **Stay Consistent:** Consistency in your actions and decisions builds confidence and stability. It shows your team they can rely on you.

The Ripple Effect of Leadership

Leadership is a privilege and a responsibility. The speed, energy, and culture of your organisation are direct reflections of you. By leading with integrity, consistency, and passion, you create a ripple effect that empowers your team to excel.

As I discuss further in this book, leadership is a lifelong journey. But remember this: the speed of the pack is determined by the leader. Set the pace, and your team will follow.

Keep the momentum, and they'll keep striving for excellence.

Action point: Write down one task that you could do next week that no one would expect you to do and then do it! Your team will be amazed and trust me their respect for you will go up. They will talk about it over lunch all week.

I remember one of my old mentors Iain Alexander doing this every year and it was amazing to watch. Every year the salesforce was set a business target, if you hit it you got to go on an amazing overseas convention, plus some other goodies.

Even though Iain was the boss of our region he qualified for the convention every year, only he wrote the business required within a week!! Locked in his glass office for us all to see. It took everyone else the best part of a year!! I never forgot it, now that's leading from the front.

Strategy 11

Reward & Recognition: The Simple Secret to Lasting Success

"People work for money but go the extra mile for recognition, praise, and rewards." - Dale Carnegie

I could write an entire book on this topic alone because it's one of the most important and, surprisingly, overlooked aspects of leadership. Recognising and rewarding people isn't just about money—it's about understanding what truly drives individuals to perform at their best.

The Power of Recognition

One of the greatest lessons I've learnt over the years is this: most people will work harder for praise and recognition than for money alone. It's an innate human need to feel valued and appreciated, and as a leader, tapping into that can transform your team.

I'll share a simple yet profound example from my time in financial services (FS). We had these little lapel pin badges—same design, different colours based on achievement levels. To an outsider, they might seem trivial, but inside the company, they were a massive deal. The pride people felt wearing those badges, especially the gold ones, was extraordinary.

When I first joined, I thought it was silly. But years later, after earning my own gold badge, I wore it with immense pride. Why? Because it symbolised recognition from my peers and leaders. It wasn't about the pin itself—it was about what it represented.

Lesson: Recognition in front of one's peers is a powerful motivator. Never underestimate the impact of acknowledging someone's hard work and accomplishments.

Big Goals, Big Rewards

If your company achieves big things, reward your team in a big way. It's not just about fairness; it's about inspiring even greater performance.

When the financial services company floated on the AIM stock market, it was a culmination of years of hard work. The founders had wisely set aside shares for directors and the sales team, based on individual performance. This was life-changing for many.

The result? A team willing to go above and beyond every single day. They believed in the vision, trusted the leadership, and knew their hard work would pay off—not just for the company, but for themselves and their families.

Lesson: If you want your team to run through brick walls for you, they need to do the following:

1. Believe in your vision.
2. Trust in your leadership.
3. See that they'll share in the success.

Practical Insights on Pay

Let's talk about money. Pay is a critical part of motivation, but it's not about just throwing money at people. It's about structuring rewards so that they align with performance and the company's success.

Why Pay Matters

If you don't pay your team enough to live a decent life, you'll never see their full potential. A stressed employee—worried about rent, bills, or groceries—cannot give their best. They're distracted, anxious, and unmotivated. While I understand cash flow can be a challenge for start-ups and small businesses, where possible, prioritise paying people a living wage. Then, layer on performance-based incentives that allow them to thrive when they excel.

If your business is based on commission only sales people make sure you create a structure where the income is unlimited. The more they do the more they earn. Do not cap it.

The Impact of Generous Rewards

My son, Oliver, who runs his own tech business, recently came full circle on this topic. Initially hesitant about paying big bonuses, he now fully embraces the philosophy. He pays his sales team well and sets substantial—but achievable—targets with significant bonuses for success. The result? A motivated, high-performing team that delivers big wins for the company and themselves.

Lesson: Well-paid, motivated people are a joy to work with. And when they succeed, you succeed.

Recognition and Cash: A Winning Combination

In my experience, a balance of recognition and financial reward is the ultimate motivator. People want to feel appreciated and valued (recognition), but they also need to see tangible benefits for their hard work (cash).

Here's a simple formula to follow:

- **Frequent, informal recognition:** Celebrate small wins regularly—public shoutouts, handwritten notes, or even just a simple "thank you."

- **Formal recognition programs:** Create structured awards for hitting specific milestones—certificates, trophies, or badges.
- **Performance-based rewards:** Tie individual and team goals to meaningful financial incentives.

Sharing the Wealth

As a leader, never forget this: when your company thrives, your team should thrive too. Sharing the wealth isn't just fair—it's smart. It builds loyalty, inspires greater effort, and ensures your team stays invested in the company's success.

When you reward and recognise your team the right way, you'll find they'll go further than you ever imagined—for themselves, for the company, and for you. Share the love, and you'll build a culture that wins.

Action point: take time out to create a reward and recognition program that is really motivational to your team but also a massive win for you and your business if targets are hit. Get creative and have fun.

Strategy 12

A Ship is Safe in the Harbour, but That's Not What Ships Were Built For

"Only those who risk going too far can possibly find out how far one can go." - T. S. Eliot

There's a fine line between kamikaze decisions and brilliance. Earlier, I advised you not to gamble everything on red or black—and I stand by that. You should never make a decision that, if it goes wrong, will sink your entire ship. But let's be clear: sometimes, when everything aligns, and you know deep in your gut that you've called it right, you have to go for it. Bold action, when backed by careful judgement, can define the difference between mediocrity and greatness.

The truth is, you will always encounter "what if" stories—opportunities you hesitated on, decisions you didn't make, risks you avoided. Regret can weigh heavier than failure, especially when you know you held back out of fear rather than sound reasoning.

The key to navigating these moments is preparation and clarity:

1. **Make decisions when you are calm.** Don't let emotions cloud your judgement or force

impulsive actions. Fear, greed, and pressure are poor advisors.

2. **Seek sound counsel.** Surround yourself with people whose opinions you trust—experienced advisors, mentors, or peers who can provide perspective. But remember, at the end of the day, it's your decision, and the responsibility rests with you.

3. **Trust your instincts.** When you've done your homework, weighed the options, and the pieces feel right, listen to your gut. It's a powerful tool shaped by your experiences and insights.

4. **Take massive action.** Once the decision is made, commit fully. Half-measures won't do. Dive in, execute with intensity, and don't allow hesitation to erode your resolve.

Consider Elon Musk's story of building Tesla—a tale that embodies risk and resilience. When Tesla faced financial collapse, Musk didn't retreat to the safety of the harbour.

Instead, he doubled down. He slept on the factory floor for weeks, solving problems in real time, refusing to let the dream die. Bankruptcy was staring him in the face, but he made a pact with himself to see it through.

His calculated gamble paid off, and today, Tesla isn't just a company—it's a global phenomenon, and Musk is one of the wealthiest individuals on the planet. If you have not heard the story about Elon sleeping on the floor, seek it out, it's truly inspiring. His belief in his company and product is a lesson learnt.

The Lesson?

Ships aren't built to stay docked. You didn't start your business, career, or journey to play it safe. Take calculated risks, lean into opportunities, and navigate the open seas with courage and conviction. Even if you fail, you'd have done so knowing you gave it everything—and that's the spirit that defines true success.

Get Ready, There Will be a Storm

Strategy 13

Keep Pumping the Pump

"Most people give up just when they're about to achieve success. They quit on the one-yard line. They give up at the last minute of the game, one foot from a winning touchdown."
- Ross Perot

Imagine one of those old-fashioned water wells you sometimes see in people's gardens—deep, dark, and seemingly endless. As a metaphor for business, I think it's absolutely perfect.

Picture this: you've been pumping and pumping the handle of this well for days, weeks, maybe even months. You're pouring your energy into it, sweating with the effort, toiling away with sheer determination and belief. You keep going, trusting that water will eventually gush out.

Now imagine the well represents something specific in your business: sales, marketing, cash flow, or any long-term goal you're striving to achieve. Day after day, you pump that metaphorical handle, only to find nothing. The well seems dry, and doubts creep in. You tell yourself, ***"There's no water in this well. I'm wasting my time. I should just give up."***

Sound familiar?

Here's the thing: sometimes the water—the

reward for all your effort—is just six inches below your line of sight. You can't see it, but it's there. You've already done the hard work. You're closer than you think. Yet, if you stop pumping, all that effort is wasted. The water level sinks back down, and you're right back where you started.

I can hear you saying, ***"Tom, I've heard this story before."*** You know what? So have I. I first heard it over 35 years ago, and it's a lesson I've never forgotten.

In business, success often comes down to belief. Do you have the belief to keep going, even when the results aren't visible? Can you stay the course when you're tired, frustrated, and tempted to walk away?

The reality is this: many people quit just before they hit water. They stop pumping the pump because the payoff seems just out of reach. But what separates those who succeed from those who don't is persistence. The willingness to keep going when others quit.

It's not about blind faith; it's about trusting the process. If you've done the groundwork, laid the right foundation, and stayed consistent, the results will come.

So, when you're on the verge of giving up, remember this metaphor. Imagine the well, the pump, and the water just out of sight. Remind yourself that all you need to do is keep pumping the pump. Success is often closer than you think.

Strategy 14

Pay Your Suppliers Early-Raving Fans

"You can have everything in life you want if you will just help enough other people get what they want." - Zig Ziglar

A good friend of mine, Martin, co-owns and manages one of the most successful financial services company in the UK, Westminster Wealth, based on Fleet Street in London.

During one of our conversations about running his business, the topic of paying company bills came up. What Martin shared with me was so unconventional, so *left field,* that it stuck with me ever since. It's advice I now give to all business owners.

As most business owners know, the common approach to paying bills is to delay them as long as possible. Sometimes, it's out of necessity due to tight cash flow, but in my experience, it's often because owners want to hold on to their cash for as long as they can.

Martin, however, does the exact opposite. He explained his ethos to me in a way that was refreshingly simple yet profound:

"Tom, if I've agreed to the terms of a deal or service with a supplier, then the money is no longer mine

once they've delivered their part of the bargain. I pay them quickly – often ahead of schedule. Why? It builds trust, creates confidence, and ensures suppliers go the extra mile for me. It also supports small businesses that might need the cash flow to stay afloat, which, in turn, benefits me. If they thrive, I thrive."

This perspective was a revelation. In a world where delayed payments are the norm, Martin's approach stood out as a model of integrity and strategic thinking. His suppliers trust him implicitly, and they reward that trust by prioritising his needs and going above and beyond to deliver exceptional service.

If your business has good cash flow, I urge you to try this strategy. Pay your suppliers early and watch how they respond. You'll be surprised by how much goodwill and loyalty it generates. Not only does it enhance your reputation as a reliable partner, it also ensures that your suppliers are more invested in your success.

Remember, strong relationships with suppliers can be one of your business's greatest assets. Treat them with respect and fairness, and they'll reward you with their best work.

Strategy 15

Buying a Company? Cut Off the Head of the Snake

"In any moment of decision, the best thing you can do is the right thing, the next best thing is the wrong thing, and the worst thing you can do is nothing." - Theodore Roosevelt

This one might sound controversial, but hear me out. I firmly believe that any deal—whether it's a merger, acquisition, or partnership—is only a good deal when it works for all parties involved.

You need to create a *win-win* scenario.

However, there are times when the success of an acquisition hinges on one critical and often uncomfortable factor: a change in leadership. In these cases, the deal won't work unless the existing leadership is replaced. These situations are delicate, complex, and sometimes messy, but necessary for the greater good.

Let me share a story from my financial services days. Our two founders decided to acquire the sales force of one of the UK's largest financial services companies. Actually, it wasn't just one sales force—it was two, operating under two distinctly separate brands. The problem? These two groups didn't like each other, and the culture within one of them was downright toxic.

The London team, while successful, was dominated by seven individuals who controlled around 200 advisers. These seven were earning a small fortune every month, largely at the expense of the advisers they managed. It quickly became clear that their interests were misaligned with ours and their advisers.

Our vision was to provide these advisers with a better, more independent home. We wanted them to become successful financial advisers with access to more options for their clients and, as a result, earn more money themselves. This would be good for the advisers and great for their clients. The clients would get better advice and products that were the best of breed.

But those seven leaders? They didn't like us, and the hostility was palpable. The acquisition was dead in the water unless we made a difficult decision. So, we did. We removed them.

It wasn't easy, and it certainly wasn't pleasant, but it was necessary. Once those individuals were out of the equation, the toxic culture dissipated, and we were able to focus on building a better environment for the majority.

The Lesson

1. **Do Your Due Diligence**: Before entering any deal, be crystal clear about what—and *who*—you're acquiring. Understanding the dynamics of leadership and culture is just as important as understanding the financials.

2. **Make Tough Decisions for the Greater Good**: Sometimes, removing a few key individuals is the only way to ensure the success of the majority. Be prepared to make unpopular decisions if it benefits the larger group.

3. **Prioritise Culture Alignment**: Toxic cultures, no matter how financially successful, can derail an acquisition. Addressing this early on can save time, money, and future headaches.

In business, as in life, not every decision is going to be popular, but sometimes the right path is the one that requires courage and clarity. Always keep the bigger picture in mind and act in the best interests of the majority, even if it means cutting off the head of the snake.

Get Ready, There Will be a Storm

Strategy 16

Politicians, Kings & Princesses

"In business, as in life, you don't get what you deserve, you get what you negotiate." - Chester L. Karrass

Over the years, I've had the good fortune to deal with a variety of influential people—politicians, royalty, and even heads of state. Most of them are incredibly gracious, warm, and welcoming.

However, one truth stands firm: everyone wants something!

Be it a new school, a state-of-the-art data centre, a medical centre of excellence, or even a contribution to an airport, the list of demands can seem endless.

These "asks" often emerge during negotiations, particularly in the world of property development. In the UK, any asks are normally negotiated upfront, overseas they normally come when you least expect them, just before you sign!

The Advice

1. **Anticipate the Ask**
If you're negotiating a planning agreement or

any large-scale project, always expect to be asked for a contribution to a "worthy cause." The request might not come upfront—it often arises once negotiations are well underway, when you're too invested to easily walk away. Be prepared for this.

2. **Lawyers Are Your Best Friend**
Ensure you have a *good* lawyer by your side throughout the process. Even more importantly, double-check every detail of the agreement yourself. Don't assume anything. Misinterpretations or inaccuracies in contracts can come back to bite you, often when it's too late to fix them.

3. **People Change When Money Is Involved**
One of the best pieces of advice I ever received came from my mentor, Bob. He once told me, "Tom, everything is great between people when it's just an idea, a concept. But watch how they change when that idea turns into real money." Bob was absolutely right. I've seen it time and again—negotiations that start

friendly and cooperative can become ugly when significant sums of money enter the equation.

4. **Keep It Clean**

Above all else, avoid backhanders or under-the-table deals. If you engage in these unethical practices, the people you're dealing with will see you as an easy target and come back for more. It's a slippery slope that can jeopardise both your integrity and your business.

Real Examples

To give you a sense of what to expect, here are some actual "asks" I've encountered during property development negotiations:

Morocco: The government requested funding for a new school in Rabat.

Anguilla: A contribution of $150,000 toward airport upgrades.

Spain: €250,000 to invest in upgrading a town square.

Thailand: Some politicians outrightly asked for personal bribes (a hard no from me).

St. Lucia: The government required funds for improvements to the island's water system.

The Moral of the Story

Negotiations with influential figures can be rewarding but also challenging. You'll need to balance diplomacy with firmness and ensure you stay within the boundaries of integrity.

Always get every agreement in writing, have it reviewed by a lawyer, and never make promises you can't—or won't—keep.

By anticipating these dynamics and preparing for them, you can navigate even the most complex negotiations with confidence.

Get Ready, There Will be a Storm

Strategy 17

Derry, the Throat-Cut Sign, and Antonio, the Baby-Faced Assassin

"You must never try to make all the money that's in a deal. Let the other fellow make some money too, because if you have a reputation for always making all the money, you won't have many deals." - J. Paul Getty

The deal is dead.

This story is one of the most intense negotiations I've ever been involved in—a lesson in composure, leverage, and having the right people in your corner.

We had spent nearly €500,000 in risk capital and 9 long months negotiating a land deal in Spain. All that stood between us and finalising the deal was a meeting to sign the agreement. It was supposed to be a formality—just signatures from the landowner, the mayor, and us. Everything was agreed upon. The town square was alive with locals, it felt like a celebration.

Our lawyer, Antonio, had flown in from Madrid specifically for this. I'd been dealing with him over the phone for months but had never met him in person. When he walked in, I was taken aback—he looked about 12 years old! But appearances can be deceiving. Despite his youthful look, Antonio turned out to be one of the sharpest negotiators I've ever worked with.

The Curveball

The signing was scheduled for 9 PM. Just before it began, Antonio came over looking serious and said, "We have a problem. The landowner is demanding another €100,000."

I was in shock. Nine months of work, half a million euros spent, and now the landowner was trying to squeeze us. I froze, unsure of what to say.

Derry, on the other hand, stayed calm. Without missing a beat, he told Antonio to bring the landowner to meet us face-to-face.

The Standoff

About 45 minutes later, Antonio returned with the landowner, a gruff and cantankerous man who seemed to relish making life difficult. Antonio explained the demand again.

Derry, with ice in his veins, asked Antonio to have the landowner look him directly in the eye. Once the landowner did, Derry calmly made a throat-cutting motion with his hand and said, "Tell him the deal is off, and we're walking."

Antonio translated, and we walked.

The Aftermath

As we walked out, I was in a complete tailspin. Had we just thrown away months of work and half a million euros?

But Derry knew exactly what he was doing. Antonio, who I now refer to as the *Baby-Faced Assassin*, stayed behind and worked his magic. By 1:30 AM, the landowner had caved. The deal was signed without the extra €100,000.

Lessons Learnt

That night taught me invaluable lessons:

1. **Control the Negotiation**
Never let emotions dictate your decisions.

Derry's calm, calculated response turned the situation in our favour. Panic achieves nothing.

2. **Leverage Matters**
By walking away, we regained control. The landowner realised he stood to lose more by not closing the deal.

3. **Surround Yourself with the Right People**
Antonio, despite his youthful appearance, was a master negotiator who understood the dynamics of the situation. Having skilled advisors is critical in high-stakes negotiations.

4. **Sometimes, You Have to Walk Away**
Knowing when to walk away is as important as knowing when to say yes. Bluffing can be powerful, but you must be prepared to follow through.

This experience reinforced my belief that negotiation is as much about psychology and preparation as it is about money. The throat-cut sign might not be in any textbook, but it worked that night—and I'll never forget it.

Strategy 18

Walking in the Shadows of Giants

"Your network is your net worth." - Porter Gale

Shayne Byrne is an Irish rugby legend, entrepreneur, and all-around incredible individual. I had the privilege of working closely with him for several years, and I can honestly say that he is one of the most inspiring, hardworking, and committed people I've ever met.

Shayne's family had a business, and he also harboured a deep passion for property and property investing. But what struck me most about him wasn't just his work ethic or his expertise—it was the respect and admiration he commanded wherever he went.

Walking Among Legends

Take a stroll down any road in Ireland with Shayne, and you'll immediately notice something extraordinary. People gravitate toward him, not just because of his rugby fame but because of the person he is. You can feel the love and respect people have for him. It's magnetic.

The Lesson

So, what's the point of this story? It's simple: seek out people like Shayne to work with.

Shayne wasn't just an incredible teammate; he was also instrumental in our business as a key introducer and leader of our distribution in Ireland. He had the ability to open doors that many couldn't. His warm referrals were pure gold—he brought us clients who trusted us instantly because they trusted him.

People like Shayne are invaluable in business. They provide what is often called a *warm referral*. Unlike cold leads, these referrals come with built-in trust because the introducer has vouched for you. This shortcut to building credibility and relationships can fast-track your success in ways few other strategies can.

Building Your Network of Giants

When looking to grow your business, prioritise finding people like Shayne—those who are respected, trusted, and deeply connected within their communities or industries. They don't just bring clients; they bring goodwill, loyalty, and opportunities you might never have accessed otherwise.

Surround yourself with people who walk in the shadows of greatness. Their influence, integrity, and trustworthiness will reflect on you and your business, just as Shayne made an immeasurable impact on ours.

Action point: Think about anyone who would make a significant difference to your business if they were associated to you in some way. It does not have to be a sports star.

Example: If you run a medical equipment business today and you want to add more credibility to your story then perhaps inviting one of the leading lights/pioneers in the sector to your advisory board would be perfect. You just need to create a win for the person that will motivate them to say yes!

Strategy 19

Good Housekeeping, Not Distrust. Get Everything in Writing

"A verbal agreement isn't worth the paper it's written on." - Ray Kroc (Founder of McDonald's Corporation)

First and foremost, having agreements in writing isn't about distrust; it's about clarity and good business practices. I encourage you to frame it this way when you approach people. Let them know that formalising the agreement is simply good housekeeping. It's a way to protect both parties and ensure that everyone understands their commitments.

In the early days of my career, I struggled with this. I loved the simplicity and honour of a handshake deal, especially with friends or trusted colleagues. But over time, I realised that avoiding written agreements wasn't fostering trust—it was leaving room for confusion, misinterpretation, and even conflict.

A written agreement serves as a single source of truth. It outlines the expectations, responsibilities, and outcomes in black and white. If something unforeseen happens—like illness, changes in the economy, or even a shift in the relationship—the agreement provides clarity when you need it most.

Believe it or not verbal agreements do stand up in court in the UK. That being said a verbal agreement is so difficult to enforce.

Why It Matters

Looking back over 30 years, I can tell you there were times when people I liked and trusted let me down. And, to be fair, there were likely times when I let others down too. Not every deal works out as planned.

- **External Factors:** The economy can tank, making a previously viable deal untenable.
- **Personal Circumstances:** Illness or unforeseen life changes can prevent someone from delivering on their part of the agreement.
- **Personality Clashes:** Sometimes, you find that you and the other party just can't work together.
- **Bad Intentions:** Unfortunately, there are

times when someone deliberately misrepresents themselves or their intentions.

Having an agreement in writing protects both parties from these. Counterintuitively, formalising an agreement can actually strengthen trust rather than weaken it. When both parties take the time to document what has been agreed upon, it shows respect for each other and for the deal. It signals a mutual commitment to transparency and accountability.

Additionally, written agreements can prevent disputes from escalating. Without one, misunderstandings often turn into conflicts. With one, you can refer back to the agreed-upon terms and resolve issues objectively, without letting emotions take over.

Final Thoughts

If you learn only one thing from this strategy, let it be this: **get everything in writing, every single time.** Even with people you trust.

Especially with people you trust. Trust is a beautiful thing, but clarity and accountability are the foundations of a lasting relationship—whether personal or professional.

Formal agreements aren't a sign of distrust; they're a way of protecting the trust you've built and ensuring that, no matter what happens, the relationship and the deal are handled with fairness and professionalism.

Action point: Review all of your important agreements verbal or otherwise, inside and outside your business. Make sure there is an up-to-date written agreement in place that reflects what has been agreed.

Strategy 20

Belt and Braces—Prepare for Illness and Unexpected Events

"By failing to prepare, you are preparing to fail." -
Benjamin Franklin

This is one of the most practical and often overlooked pieces of advice for business owners. The unpredictability of life—illness, accidents, or even untimely death—can have catastrophic consequences not only for you but also for your business, your partners, and your family.

Let me share some examples and lessons to illustrate why it's crucial to have a "belt and braces" approach to protect what you've built.

Case 1: The Sole Proprietor's Story

John, a great guy I worked with, was the life and soul of the party, an outstanding professional, and a joy to be around. He was self-employed, running his business under my umbrella, and was as reliable as they come.

One day, out of the blue, John asked to grab a quick beer after work. When I saw his face, I knew something was wrong.

That evening, he told me he had been diagnosed with terminal cancer and was given just 6–12 months to live. It was a shocking, humbling moment. The good news for John and his family was that he had planned ahead. He had insurance that supported his family while he was ill and a life policy that took care of them after he passed.

John's story taught me a valuable lesson: even when things are going well, life can throw you a curveball. He used his business to protect his family, ensuring they were secure even in the worst-case scenario.

At Christmas this year (2024), I listened to the amazing Olympian Chris Hoy. Chris was diagnosed last year with terminal cancer.

I was so taken aback it was tough to listen to. I thought, "Why has this lovely guy just got dealt such a shitty hand?" One of the best athletes/cyclists of all time.

There of course is no rhyme or reason. Chris's wife is also poorly, I wish them both the best for 2025.

The Lesson:

- Plan for the unexpected.
- Set aside a portion of your revenue to invest in protection, such as critical illness cover and life insurance.
- Do it now – don't wait until it's too late.

Case 2: The Business Partners' Dilemma

Let's talk about Susan and Jane, two business partners who co-owned Rainbow Corp. Ltd. (made-up names). They had a solid partnership, a thriving business, and a clear mutual understanding – or so they thought.

One day, Susan was diagnosed with a severe illness. She informed Jane that she needed to step back to focus on her health. Jane assured her that she would hold the fort, and she meant it. But as Susan's condition worsened, Jane found herself overwhelmed. She needed to hire someone to fill Susan's role, which stretched the business's finances.

Questions quickly arose:

- How long should Jane keep paying Susan if she can't contribute?
- Could Jane afford to buy Susan out?
- Did Susan even want to sell her shares?
- If Susan passed away, did Jane want Susan's husband as her new business partner?

The situation became even more complicated when Susan passed away. Her shares were inherited by her husband, who had no experience in the business. Jane was left with an unworkable situation, unable to move forward without resolving the ownership issue.

The Solution:

- **Start with the end in mind.** When you go into business with someone, plan for worst-case scenarios from day one.

- **Update your Memorandum and Articles of Association.** These documents should clearly outline what happens in the event of long-term illness or death of a partner.
- **Draft a shareholders' agreement.** This should specify buyout terms, valuation methods, and procedures to ensure a smooth transition.

Practical Steps to Protect Your Business

1. **Seek Legal Advice:**

Hire a lawyer to draft or update your Memorandum and Articles of Association and shareholders' agreement. These documents should include clauses for:

- Long-term illness.
- Death of a partner.
- Buyout mechanisms and valuation terms.

2. **Secure Insurance Cover:**

Work with a corporate financial adviser to create an insurance plan tailored to your business.

Examples include:

- **Critical illness cover:** Provides income if a partner or key team member is incapacitated.
- **Life insurance for buy-sell agreements:** Ensures funds are available to buy out a deceased partner's shares, so their family receives the value in cash rather than ownership.

3. **Fund Through the Business:**
Many premiums can be structured as a business expense, potentially offering tax advantages (consult a tax adviser to confirm).

4. **Have Regular Check-Ins:**
Circumstances change. Review your agreements and insurance policies regularly to ensure they still meet your needs.

Final Word

No one likes to think about illness or death, but failing to plan for these possibilities can lead to chaos, financial ruin, and broken relationships.

Taking the time to implement "belt and braces" measures now will give you peace of mind and ensure your business, partners, and family are protected no matter what life throws at you.

Don't wait. Start today.

Action point: seek out professional independent advise. Your accountant or business coach (if you have one) might also have experience in this area. This can be a very touchy area for business partners as well as your spouse so please take your time and explain things clearly. Others need to know you have their best interests in mind.

Strategy **21**

Turn Your Business into a McDonald's —Systemise for Success

"Systems run the business, and people run the systems." - Michael Gerber (Author of the E-Myth Revisited)

One of the first things I focus on when working with a new client is their systems—how things run, who does what, and how well processes are documented.

For most small businesses, especially those under £10 million in turnover, growth happens organically. The business often evolves without much formal structure, relying on the hard work and adaptability of the team.

In the early years, it's "all hands on deck." Employees and directors often wear multiple hats, handling two or three roles at once. Over time, as the business grows, the team expands, revenues increase, and things start running smoothly. People settle into their roles, becoming experts in their areas and vital to the business's success. However, in many cases, there's a glaring issue: the lack of written processes and systems.

From my experience, only a handful of business owners have a comprehensive, written system for every aspect of their business. This oversight can cost you dearly.

The Case for Systemising Your Business

Here are four compelling reasons to turn your business into a well-oiled machine, like McDonald's:

1. Protect Against the Loss of Key Team Members

Imagine if one of your top employees—a person who knows your operations inside and out—resigns tomorrow. They'll walk out the door with a treasure trove of knowledge that you've paid for but don't own. Without documented processes, that knowledge is gone forever, leaving you scrambling to fill the void.

2. Increase the Value of Your Business

Businesses with robust processes, systems, and data are far more attractive to potential buyers. A company that runs on systems rather than personalities signals to a buyer that it's scalable, transferable, and resilient. Buyers aren't just purchasing your current profits; they're buying the ease with which those profits can grow.

3. Improve Team Management and Accountability

Having detailed systems fosters transparency. It shows your team that you're serious about the business's success and, by extension, their success. Regularly updated processes also help you keep a finger on the pulse of every key area, ensuring you're managing effectively and spotting potential issues before they escalate.

4. Simplify Onboarding and Training

When you bring on a new team member or promote someone to a leadership role, a clear, detailed roadmap makes their transition seamless. Instead of relying on guesswork or endless questions, they can hit the ground running. This saves time, reduces errors, and builds confidence in new hires.

The McDonald's Mindset: Build a System-Driven Business

McDonald's is a global success not because they sell the best burgers but because of their systems. Their processes are so detailed and consistent that a Big Mac tastes the same whether you're in London or Los Angeles. This consistency doesn't happen by chance—it's the result of meticulous documentation, training, and adherence to processes.

Action point: Here's how you can emulate that approach in your own business:

Step 1: Call a Team Meeting
Explain to your team why this initiative is critical. Share the four points above to get buy-in and help them understand the long-term benefits—for the business and for them.

Step 2: Assign Documentation Tasks
Give each team member a month to document their role in detail. This should include:

- What they do daily, weekly, and monthly.

- How they perform their tasks, step by step.
- The tools and resources they use.
- Common challenges and how they resolve them.

Step 3: Review and Consolidate

Once everyone has submitted their documents, review them for clarity and completeness. Consolidate them into a central repository—a shared folder, software system, or operations manual—that everyone can access.

Step 4: Keep the Documentation Alive

Processes and roles evolve over time. Schedule periodic reviews—quarterly or annually—to update the documentation. Make this part of your company culture.

The Golden Result

By systemising your business, you create a scalable, resilient operation that can weather challenges and grow without constant oversight. These documents become your business's "gold dust," ensuring:

- Continuity during transitions or unexpected departures.
- Confidence from investors, buyers, and partners.
- Efficiency in onboarding new team members.
- A culture of clarity, accountability, and professionalism.

Be like McDonald's. Build a business that runs on systems, not just people. You'll thank yourself—and so will your team, clients, and future buyers.

Get Ready, There Will be a Storm

Strategy 22

Chet Holmes the Legend: How to Manage Multiple Businesses and Personalities at the Same Time

"The missing ingredient for nearly all of the 1,000+ clients I have worked with directly to improve their businesses is pig-headed discipline and determination." - Chet Holmes

When I was running 12 companies, I can remember feeling like I was being pulled in every direction, organised chaos. Something needed to change but I was not sure what. How was I going to expand?

I had a first-class PA called Anne who had been with me for years but I was still struggling. And then I read Chet's book and at that time it changed my life.

I am delighted to share Chet's strategy for time management with you and I fully recommend you buy his book, "The Ultimate Sales Machine."

In **"The Ultimate Sales Machine,"** Chet Holmes introduces a time management formula designed to enhance productivity and effectively manage multiple projects simultaneously. This approach, known as the "Time Management Secrets of Billionaires," comprises six key steps:

1. **Touch It Once:** Address tasks immediately upon encountering them to prevent the inefficiency of revisiting them multiple times. For instance, when handling emails, decide promptly whether to respond, delegate, or schedule time to address them later.

2. **List the Top Six Priorities:** Each day, create a list of the six most important tasks that will yield the highest results. Concentrate on completing these items to maintain focus on critical objectives.

3. **Allocate Time for Each Task:** Estimate the duration required for each task and adhere to this timeframe. This practice ensures efficient time utilisation and prevents tasks from extending beyond their necessary scope.

4. **Plan the Day:** Dedicate the initial moments of your day to organise and prioritise tasks. This proactive planning sets a structured agenda, enabling a more focused and productive workflow.

5. **Prioritise Tasks:** Identify and tackle the most challenging or significant tasks first. Addressing high-priority items early in the day leverages peak energy levels and sets a positive tone for the remainder of the day.

6. **Establish Efficient Transitions:** Minimise downtime between tasks to maintain momentum and reduce productivity losses. Streamlining transitions helps in sustaining focus and achieving more within the available time.

By implementing these steps, individuals can enhance their time management skills, leading to increased productivity and more effective handling of multiple projects concurrently.

Chet advocates for a disciplined approach, suggesting that dedicating specific blocks of time to each project can enhance productivity and ensure consistent progress. By allocating focused periods—such as an hour or two—to individual tasks or business areas, you can maintain momentum across various initiatives without becoming overwhelmed. This method allows for deep concentration, reduces the inefficiencies associated with multitasking, and ensures that each endeavour receives the attention it deserves. His strategy underscores the value of structured time management in achieving business success.

Chet passed too early, the man was widely recognised as the best of the best at his skill set in the US.*

Action point: Take time out to review how you are currently managing projects, people and your own time. Reengineer your time management and how you prioritise projects. Then stick to your new plan!! (The hard part for most) Remember to allocate quality time to your loved ones.

*Chet Holmes passed away at the age of **55** on **August 12, 2012**. He died from complications related to **acute myeloid leukaemia (AML)**, a type of blood cancer.

Strategy 23

Why Do Robbers Rob Banks? Because That's Where the Money Is

"Opportunities multiply as they are seized."
- Sun Tzu (The Art of War)

This concept is deceptively simple yet critically important for any business owner: focus your efforts – and your sales team's energy – on the areas that bring the highest returns. It's a principle that's often overlooked in the hustle of daily operations, especially during periods of growth. But ignoring it can lead to wasted time, lost profits, and even missed opportunities.

Understand Your Sales Landscape

The first step in applying this strategy is to get crystal clear on your sales data. Ask yourself:

- **What are your top-performing products or services?**

Which offerings bring in the highest revenue and profit margins? Also, add new products and services that your clients will want to buy.

- **What is underperforming?**

Are there products or services that are breaking even – or worse, losing money?

- **How much time and effort are your sales team spending on each offering?**

Are they chasing low-value deals while neglecting higher-value opportunities?

Without this level of clarity, you're essentially flying blind. You could be directing resources toward unprofitable areas without even realising it.

Perform a Root-and-Branch Sales Audit

Here's how to dig deep into your sales processes:

1. Analyse Sales Performance by Product/Service

Break down your revenue and profitability by product or service. Identify which offerings are generating the lion's share of your profits and which are dragging you down.

2. Evaluate Your Sales Funnel

Examine your sales pipeline from start to finish. Where are leads coming from? How are they being qualified? Are there bottlenecks or inefficiencies in the process?

3. Review Time Allocation

Look at how your sales team spends their time. Are they prioritising high-value opportunities? If not, why? It could be a lack of training, unclear goals, or outdated incentives.

4. Challenge the Status Quo

It's easy to fall into the trap of "we've always done it this way." But just because a particular product or service has been part of your line-up for years doesn't mean it still deserves a place. If it's not contributing to your bottom line, it's time to rethink its role in your business.

Focus on the Money

Once you've identified where the money is, shift your strategy to maximise those opportunities:

1. Double Down on Profitable Offerings

Invest more resources—time, marketing, and

training—into the products or services that generate the most profit. This might mean expanding your reach, enhancing your offerings, or refining your pitch.

2. Cut or Transform Underperformers

For products or services that aren't delivering, you have two choices: improve them or eliminate them. If they can't be made profitable, they're a drain on your resources and focus.

3. Align Your Sales Team's Goals

Ensure your sales team is incentivised to focus on high-value opportunities. Adjust their KPIs to reflect profitability, not just volume.

4. Stay Close to the Data

Make it a habit to review your sales stats regularly—monthly at an absolute minimum. This keeps you connected to the realities of your business and allows you to spot trends and opportunities early.

Why Robbers Rob Banks (David Tuson)

The phrase "Why do robbers rob banks? Because that's where the money is," serves as a sharp reminder: focus your efforts where the rewards are greatest. In business, this means putting your time, energy, and resources into areas that drive profitability and growth.

By continuously refining your sales approach, staying close to your data, and focusing on high-value opportunities, you'll not only maximise your profits but also build a leaner, more effective sales machine.

Stay vigilant, stay focused, and always remember: in business, like in heists, the biggest returns come from knowing exactly where the money is – and going after it.

Strategy 24

Financial Audit: Cut Costs, Boost Value and Strengthen Your Business

"Cutting costs without improving the customer experience is a race to the bottom. But cutting waste while increasing value is a race to the top." - Jeff Bezos

Conducting regular financial audits is one of the simplest yet most powerful strategies for improving the financial health and value of your business. Every pound you save by cutting unnecessary costs or optimising your expenses flows straight to your bottom line—and can significantly impact your company's valuation.

Why Regular Financial Audits Are Essential

1. You're Likely Overpaying
Many businesses are spending money unnecessarily, whether it's for services, subscriptions, or lending terms that are no longer competitive. What made sense a year or two ago may now be outdated or overpriced.

2. Borrowing Costs Are a Hidden Drain
If your business relies on loans or financing, the terms you agreed to when you needed funding may not be the best option anymore. Refinancing or renegotiating with lenders can free up significant cash flow.

3. Cash Flow is the Lifeline of Your Business

If cash flow is tight, you may feel trapped. However, creative solutions often exist—better financing terms, asset-based lending, or more favourable vendor agreements—that can ease the strain without additional borrowing.

The Big Picture: Profits Drive Value

Let's look at a case study: **XYZ Inc.**

- Turnover: £3 million
- Profit: £1 million/year
- Valuation Multiple: 10x profits
- Estimated Sale Value: £10 million

The owners of XYZ Inc. conducted a detailed financial audit. They realised they were overpaying for numerous services and financing arrangements. By becoming more efficient, they saved £200k annually, raising their profit to £1.2 million.

- New Profit: £1.2 million/year
- New Valuation at 10x: £12 million

This seemingly small change in efficiency increased the company's value by **£2 million**!

How to Conduct a Financial Audit

1. Review All Expenditures
Audit every expense in your business, from utility bills to office supplies. Are there cheaper or better alternatives?

2. **Reassess Subscriptions and Services**
Check recurring costs such as software subscriptions, consultants, and professional services. Are you still using everything you're paying for?

3. **Renegotiate Vendor Agreements**
Speak with your suppliers and negotiate better terms. Often, long-standing relationships can yield discounts if you ask.

4. **Evaluate Financing Terms**
Work with a financial adviser or broker to review your loans or credit lines. Could you

refinance for a lower rate or more favourable terms?

5. **Examine Operating Efficiencies**
Streamline your processes to reduce waste. Even small improvements can add up over time.

The Role of Advisers

A skilled **broker** or **corporate financial adviser** can uncover hidden opportunities. They often know of financial tools, funding sources, or creative arrangements you may not have considered. Their expertise can be invaluable, especially for businesses navigating cash flow challenges or looking to sell.

Action Point: Take Control of Your Financial Efficiency

Step 1: Conduct a 30-Day Cost Audit
Review every business expense—**subscriptions, vendor contracts, operational costs, and financing terms.**

Identify waste, redundancy, or outdated expenses that no longer serve your company's goals.

Step 2: Implement Cost-Cutting Without Sacrificing Value

Eliminate or replace unnecessary expenditures, but ensure that cost-cutting doesn't harm **customer experience, employee productivity, or long-term growth.**

Step 3: Renegotiate & Optimise Financial Commitments

Engage with **lenders, suppliers, and service providers** to negotiate better terms, lower interest rates, and improved pricing structures. Leverage long-term relationships for cost reductions.

Step 4: Strengthen Cash Flow & Business Value

Ensure you have the right financing structure in place to **maximise liquidity and long-term financial health.** Regularly reassess borrowing terms, payment cycles, and asset utilisation.

Step 5: Set a Recurring Financial Review

Financial audits should be a **quarterly or biannual practice**, not a one-time effort. Assign a dedicated person or team to continually **evaluate expenses, renegotiate contracts, and seek operational efficiencies.**

By making financial audits a **habit**, you ensure your business stays lean, profitable, and primed for growth.

Get Ready, There Will be a Storm

Strategy 25

Databases/CRM: Building the Foundation for Business Growth and Efficiency

"The goal is to turn data into information, and information into insight." - Carly Fiorina (Former CEO of Hewlett-Packard)

If your business isn't leveraging a CRM (Customer Relationship Management) system, it's time to make the switch.

Far too often, I meet business owners who are still relying on Excel spreadsheets or scattered records to manage customer and contact data. While it may feel familiar or cost-effective, this approach is both inefficient and limiting to growth.

A CRM is more than a tool—it's a strategic asset that can transform how your business operates, engages with customers, and scales. Data more than ever drives valuations.

Why Every Business Needs a CRM

1. Increases Business Valuation

A well-maintained CRM system adds measurable value to your business. Why?

- **Potential acquirers love data.** Businesses with organised, clean, and actionable customer data are far more appealing during acquisition talks.

- CRMs demonstrate that your business is well-run and scalable.

2. Speeds Up Due Diligence

- During a sale or fundraising process, buyers and investors will demand detailed customer and operational information.
- A CRM allows you to quickly provide accurate reports on customer metrics, sales pipelines, churn rates, and other key data points. This transparency reduces the time and friction involved in due diligence.

3. Facilitates Upselling and Cross-Selling

- Mining your existing customer base for new sales opportunities becomes effortless.
- With the insights a CRM provides, you can identify patterns, preferences, and upselling opportunities.

4. Improves Conversion Rates

- For prospects who haven't yet converted, a CRM helps track where they are in the sales funnel.
- Automated follow-ups, segmentation, and targeted communications increase the likelihood of turning leads into customers.

5. Streamlines Marketing Efforts

- Tools like Smartlead.ai, Mailchimp, HubSpot, or ActiveCampaign integrate seamlessly with most CRMs.
- You can segment customers and prospects for personalised marketing campaigns that drive engagement and results.

6. Enhances Team Management

- A good CRM provides clear visibility into team activities and performance.
- Managers can track sales progress, identify bottlenecks, and coach team members more effectively.

7. Boosts Sales Productivity

- CRMs eliminate the chaos of sticky notes, spreadsheets, and scattered files.
- Sales teams have everything they need in one place: lead details, customer history, and follow-up reminders.
- Automating repetitive tasks allows your salespeople to focus on what they do best—selling!!

Choosing the Right CRM for Your Business

There are many CRM platforms available, ranging from free or entry-level options to enterprise-grade solutions.

Key Considerations:

- Ease of use: A CRM is only effective if your team actually uses it.
- Scalability: Choose a system that can grow with your business.
- Integration: Make sure it works with tools you're already using, like your email, accounting software, or marketing

platforms.

Getting Started: Implementing a CRM

1. **Assess Your Needs:**
    - Do you want to improve sales tracking, customer service, or marketing?
    - Identify the key challenges your CRM needs to address. Map this out with your team before you start evaluating

2. **Clean Your Data:**
    - Before migrating from Excel or other tools, clean up your existing data.
    - Remove duplicates, update outdated information, and standardise formats.

3. **Train Your Team:**
    - Invest time in training your staff to use the CRM effectively.
    - Highlight how it will make their jobs easier and improve results.

4. **Automate Where Possible:**
   - Use automation for tasks like follow-up emails, pipeline updates, and reminders.
   - Set up workflows that reduce manual effort and ensure consistency.

5. **Regularly Audit and Optimise:**
   - Schedule regular check-ins to ensure your CRM is meeting business needs.
   - Update processes and features as your business evolves.

The Payoff

Transitioning to a CRM might seem like a big step, because at first it is damn time-consuming, but the benefits are undeniable.

It's not just about organising data—it's about empowering your business to operate smarter, sell better, and grow faster. Whether you're looking to improve day-to-day efficiency or prepare for a future sale, a CRM is one of the best investments you can make.

As the saying goes: "You can't manage what you don't measure." A CRM helps you measure and manage every critical aspect of your customer relationships, ensuring long-term success.

Strategy 26

You Are Going To Need A Bigger Boat-Raising Money from Investors

"The biggest mistake a small business can make is to think like a small business." - Michael E. Gerber (Author of the E-Myth Revisited)

Raising money from equity Investors? Trust me you are going to need more than you think. If you're unfamiliar with the phrase "You're going to need a bigger boat," let me explain.

In the classic film Jaws, there's a pivotal scene where the seasoned fisherman, Quint, and the police chief, Brody, are out hunting for the shark. Quint is an expert—he's caught plenty of sharks before. But when he finally lays eyes on Jaws, he's visibly stunned. This isn't just any shark—it's massive, far bigger than anything he's ever encountered.

In that moment, reality hits, and he turns to Brody and delivers the now-iconic line:
"You're gonna need a bigger boat."

It's a brilliant metaphor—one that has since become shorthand for realising that your original plan, resources, or expectations are simply not enough for the challenge ahead.

And when it comes to raising money from investors? Trust me—you're going to need a bigger boat.

In my online course, Capital Catalyst: **Mastering the Art of Fundraising for Founders (www.tom-capital.co.uk),** I dedicate an entire section to this critical topic.

Each of the 12 modules includes a powerful, thought-provoking exercise that must be completed before advancing to the next stage.

My promise to every founder: Follow the plan without deviation, and in just 30 days, you'll be fully prepared to raise the capital your business needs.

Here is an excerpt and exercise from one of the modules.

Critical Exercise: Assessing Your True Funding Needs

Before moving on to Module 3, take a full day to carefully assess how much funding you actually need. Most founders underestimate their financial requirements and overestimate how quickly revenue will come in—this exercise is designed to prevent that mistake.

Ask yourself:

- If you're serious about growth, how many new staff will you realistically need?
- Will you require new equipment or technology?
- Do you need a larger office, warehouse, or production space?
- Are your marketing costs likely to be higher than expected?

If you are buying a new business, are you sure you are raising enough to acquire the business as well as invest in the business?

Are you allowing for wage increases?

How about increased production costs?

Go deep. Be brutally honest with yourself. Drill down into the numbers and get forensic.

12-Month Financial Reality Check

- Strip your business down to the essentials and map out the next 12 months in detail.
- Pay yourself properly—this isn't about scraping by; you need financial stability to lead effectively.
- Reduce your sales forecasts by 25%—optimism is great, but revenue often takes longer than expected.
- Examine your payment cycles—how quickly do clients actually pay you? 30 days? 60? Some businesses wait 90+ days for payment, and it kills their cash flow.

Build a Financial Safety Net

- Always have contingency funds—unforeseen expenses will arise, and having reserves can be the difference between survival and collapse.
- Cashflow is king. A lack of working

capital can kill a business before it even gets airborne. Review, review, review.

The Harsh Truth

Once you complete this exercise, you'll likely realise you need more money than you initially thought. If you estimated £200k, you probably need £300k. This isn't about raising excess cash—it's about avoiding financial strain and setting yourself up for success.

Get Input from Your Inner Circle

If you have trusted business partners or senior management, involve them in this process. Fresh perspectives often reveal blind spots you may have missed.

This exercise is non-negotiable. Take the time to do it thoroughly before progressing. Your future success depends on it.

Strategy **27**

Always Have Two Business Banks

"Do not put all your eggs in one basket." - Warren Buffett

BETTER TO BE SAFE THAN SORRY

This strategy might seem unnecessary—until the day you need it.

Having two business banking relationships is like having an insurance policy for your financial operations. I learnt this lesson first-hand, thanks to sage advice from David Tuson, who warned me about the risks of relying entirely on one bank. At the time, I didn't fully grasp the importance of his words, but when the moment of truth came, I realised how critical this advice was.

Why You Need Two Banks

1. Diversification Reduces Risk

Banks are businesses, and like any business, they have their own policies, priorities, and appetite for risk. If you fall on hard times, your primary bank may suddenly become unsupportive—even if you've been a loyal customer for years.

- Having a second bank gives you flexibility and leverage when you need it most.

- If one bank changes its terms or denies your requests, the other can serve as a lifeline.

2. Protect Against "All Eggs in One Basket"

When all your loans, overdrafts, and operating accounts are with one bank, that bank effectively controls your business's financial oxygen. If they decide to tighten the tap, your business could suffocate. A second bank prevents this single point of failure.

3. Improved Negotiating Power

Having relationships with two banks means neither one can take you for granted. If you need a loan, better terms on an overdraft, or flexibility on a facility, you can leverage your dual relationships to negotiate more favourable terms.

4. Operational Continuity

Imagine your primary bank experiences a major outage, fraud investigation, or other disruption. Having a secondary bank account ensures your business can continue to operate without grinding to a halt.

My Experience: A Lesson Learnt

When I set up a new business structure, I took David's advice and opened accounts with two banks. At the time, it seemed unnecessary – an extra admin hassle. But when the business hit a rough patch, my primary bank became inflexible and unsupportive, despite the substantial funds that had flowed through their system over the years.

We survived because we had two banks.

Strategy 28

Seek Out Professionals Who Get You and Care

"Teamwork is the ability to work together toward a common vision. The ability to direct individual accomplishments toward organisational objectives. It is the fuel that allows common people to attain uncommon results." - Dale Carnegie

Your business success isn't just about what you do; it's also about who you surround yourself with. The professionals you choose to support your journey—accountants, lawyers, brokers, and advisors—aren't just service providers; they are critical allies who can make or break your ability to thrive.

Why Relationships with Professionals Matter

1. They Keep Your Business Running Smoothly

Professionals who care about you and your business will go beyond the minimum. They'll proactively look for ways to save you time and money, protect you from risks, and provide you with the best tools, services, or deals.

2. They Respond Quickly in Times of Crisis

When challenges arise, you don't want someone who treats you as just another client. A professional who truly gets you will prioritise your needs and respond swiftly, helping you resolve problems with as little disruption as possible.

3. They'll Go the Extra Mile

Whether it's negotiating better terms, finding hidden opportunities, or connecting you with useful contacts, a professional who cares will go above and beyond to support your success.

4. Trust Enhances Efficiency

A strong, trust-based relationship allows you to focus on growing your business without constantly worrying about whether your advisors have your best interests at heart.

Building Relationships with Professionals

Choosing the right professionals takes effort, but it's worth it. Here's how to approach it:

1. Choose Carefully and Take Your Time

- Look beyond qualifications and experiences.
- Assess their communication style, problem-solving approach, and level of enthusiasm for working with you.
- Where possible, get recommendations from trusted contacts.

2. Meet Face-to-Face

Meeting in person allows both parties to connect on a deeper level. It helps them understand your goals, challenges, and values—and gives you insight into their personality and work ethic.

3. Build Rapport Outside the Office

If budgets allow, take the time to meet for lunch or a drink in a more relaxed setting. Ask about their hobbies, family, and interests. Finding common ground can help strengthen your connection, making the relationship more enjoyable and productive. For example, if you play golf, and they play golf. Not only is it fun but you get to chat for 4 hours. This is a great time to get to know someone and vice versa.

4. Focus on Alignment

- Look for professionals whose values align with yours.
- Make sure they understand your ambitions and vision for the future.
- Work with people who genuinely care about your success, not just their fee.

Key Professionals to Consider

Here are some of the key professionals who can make a significant impact on your business:

1. **Accountant**: Beyond taxes, a good accountant can provide insights into profitability, cash flow, and growth strategies. They can also be your first port of call if you need to value your business.

2. **Lawyer**: An experienced business lawyer can protect your interests in contracts, disputes, and intellectual property matters. Also, I have found that people take you more seriously if you have good lawyers.

3. **Finance Broker**: Helps you secure the best financing options, whether it's for growth, acquisitions, or managing cash flow.

4. **Independent Financial Adviser**: Assists with personal and business financial planning, ensuring you and your business are protected.

5. Property Consultant: If your business involves real estate, having an expert to advise on leases, purchases, and valuations can save you a fortune. You will also need a good conveyancer if you get involved in property transactions.

Final Thoughts

The people you work with directly influence your business's success. Choose professionals who not only understand your needs but also share your commitment to excellence. By building strong, mutually beneficial relationships, you'll have a team of experts who'll help you navigate challenges, capitalise on opportunities, and take your business to new heights.

Remember: The right professionals are an investment in your future, not just an expense. Choose wisely!

Strategy 29

Train Your Sales Team as If Your Life Depended on It

"You don't build a business. You build people, and then people build the business." - Zig Ziglar

'We are going to drill this until you you can do it in your sleep.

Sales are the lifeblood of every business, yet so many companies let this critical area underperform due to poor training, weak senior management, or lack of motivation. The story I'm about to share highlights why investing in your sales team is non-negotiable if you want to succeed.

The Audi Experience: A Case Study in Lost Sales

Recently, my partner Jo and I decided to purchase a new family car.

After some research, we settled for the Audi Q4, an electric 4x4 priced at £55,000. Excited about our choice, we walked into the local Audi dealership ready to buy.

Our first interaction with the staff was promising. A polite and professional lady greeted us, offered us drinks, and asked if we wanted assistance or were just browsing. It was a strong start.

Unfortunately, things quickly went downhill from there.

Where It All Went Wrong:

1. **Long, Unnecessary Wait:** The salesperson assigned to us wasn't busy but still made us wait longer than was reasonable.

2. **Disinterest and Lack of Focus:** When he finally spoke with us, he seemed distracted and disengaged, leaving us feeling unimportant.

3. **Terrible Test Drive:** Instead of allowing us a meaningful drive to truly experience the car, he insisted on accompanying us for a short 5–7-minute loop.

4. **Zero Sales Pitch:** When Jo asked, "Sell me the car; what's great about it?" the salesperson, despite four years in the role, had nothing compelling to say.

We left feeling disappointed and irritated, despite really liking the car itself.

Jo ended up calling a salesperson from another dealership – someone who had impressed her years ago – and we bought the car through him instead.

The local salesperson lost a significant sale and commission, and Audi Leicester lost a customer.

Why This Happens: The Core Issues

From years of experience training thousands of salespeople, I've identified three primary reasons for poor sales performance:

1. Poor Training and Ongoing Development
Salespeople must be equipped with product knowledge, customer service skills, and a compelling pitch. This doesn't happen automatically; it requires structured training and regular refreshers to ensure they stay sharp.

2. Poor Management and Leadership

A disinterested or absent leader results in a demotivated team. Strong sales managers set the tone, monitor performance, and lead by example, ensuring everyone is accountable and driven to excel.

3. Lack of Motivation

Motivation isn't about using a stick-and-carrot approach. Salespeople thrive when they feel valued, supported, and appreciated. A simple "well done" or a public acknowledgment of their efforts can go a long way in keeping morale high.

How to Train a World-Class Sales Team

If you want your sales team to deliver exceptional results consistently, here's how to make it happen:

1. Prioritise Training and Development
Show them, don't tell them. Go first.

- **Initial Training:** Cover product knowledge, sales techniques, and customer care.

- **Ongoing Development:** Regularly refresh their skills with workshops, role-playing exercises, and updated sales strategies.
- **Drill the Basics:** Ensure every salesperson knows their pitch and can deliver it flawlessly.

2. Focus on Leadership

- Appoint leaders who care about their team's success.
- Monitor performance, provide constructive feedback, and be present in the day-to-day activities of the sales floor.
- Lead by example: demonstrate enthusiasm, resilience, and commitment.

3. Cultivate a Motivational Environment

- **Catch Them Doing Things Right:** Acknowledge and reward good performance, even with small gestures.
- **Provide Immediate Feedback:** Correct mistakes quickly to prevent bad habits.

- **Foster Healthy Competition:** Introduce friendly contests or recognition programs to keep the team engaged.

Final Thoughts

The Audi Leicester experience is a cautionary tale. Despite significant resources, they lost a £55,000 sale due to preventable mistakes. Now, imagine if every salesperson in your team delivered subpar service, what would that cost your business?

Sales training isn't optional; it's a critical investment in your business's future.

Ensure your team is well-trained, motivated, and led by someone who genuinely cares about their success.

Strategy 30

Polar Explorer Robert Swan and the Russian

"Diversity is being invited to the party; inclusion is being asked to dance." - Verna Myers

Many years ago, I had the privilege of attending an event where the guest speaker was the renowned polar explorer, Robert Swan.

Robert had authored a book titled, *"Antarctica 2041: My Quest to Save the Earth's Last Wilderness."* In it, he recounts his incredible adventures, including his historic feat as the first person to walk to both the North and South Poles.

The book also highlights his passionate mission to preserve Antarctica and raise awareness about the pressing issue of climate change.

Robert was captivating, sharing profound insights into his journey, mission, and vision for the future. Yet, what resonated most with me was the story of Sasha, the Russian member of his polar expedition team.

Before beginning their trek, the team was forced to endure nearly 6 months confined to their cabin during the Antarctic winter. Extreme weather conditions and the unrelenting darkness of the polar winter made travel impossible, testing the team's patience, camaraderie, and mental fortitude. This prolonged isolation became a defining moment, demanding extraordinary levels of discipline, adaptability, and conflict resolution to maintain morale.

Sasha, however, frustrated many of the team members during this time. Let's just say he wasn't the most popular guy. He was eccentric—washing naked in the snow every day (a habit we now recognise as beneficial to health)—and his personality rubbed some people the wrong way.

Here's the twist: despite his quirks and the friction he caused, Robert Swan never lost faith in Sasha. Sasha's sole job on the expedition was to navigate the team to the pole with absolute precision. In the brutal conditions of Antarctica, being even one degree off course would have meant death.

When the time finally came to leave the cabin, Sasha proved to be the team's most invaluable asset. His skill, focus, and unwavering determination got them to the pole. By the end of the journey, Sasha—who had once frustrated the group—was universally admired and loved.

The Takeaway

Find people who can make a massive difference to your business and your team. They don't need to be universally liked, but they must have integrity, a good heart, and the ability to deliver results. Their value may not always be immediately obvious, but in the critical moments, they'll prove indispensable.

Strategy 31

Daily Habits – The Foundation Stone of Success

"We are what we repeatedly do. Excellence, then, is not an act, but a habit." – Aristotle

If there's one game-changer in business and life, it's your daily habits and routines.

Creating a winning routine that you live by is the most important key to success. For those who have worked with me or listened to me speak over the years, you know I have always been big on goals. I still am.

However, as I've grown older, I've realised that the real key to success isn't just setting goals—it's being consistent. Daily actions compound over time, shaping your future. Without consistency, achieving your goals becomes nearly impossible.

The Power of Consistency

The world's most successful entrepreneurs, investors, and leaders attribute their achievements to disciplined daily habits. And guess what? Most of them are incredibly happy and live enriched lives—there's a clue in that!

Take a moment to reflect on a time in the past when you were at the top of your game—when business was thriving, and it seemed like everything you touched turned to gold. Without realising it, you had great daily habits, a structured routine, and you were in flow.

Most people act out these habits unconsciously when things are going well. They don't think, they just do, and that's great. The problem comes when a storm arrives. The same person is no longer consciously focused on their daily rituals, and things start to go wrong, sometimes spiralling out of control.

It's the consistency of thoughts, actions, and focus that helps the best navigate through storms.

The Success Formula: Habits + Time = Transformation

Imagine habits as the bricks of a house and discipline as the cement. Without solid daily routines, the foundation of success collapses under pressure.

A tiny improvement every day (1%) can lead to astonishing growth over time due to the compounding effect. This is why habits matter more than motivation—because motivation fades, but habits sustain.

In his brilliant book ***Atomic Habits***, James Clear explains that if you improve by just 1% every day, you'll be 37 times better in a year. This principle highlights the power of small, consistent improvements. It's a fantastic read, and I highly recommend it.

The Key Areas of Daily Habits for Success

To make this practical, let's break it down into five essential areas of daily routines that high achievers follow:

1. Mindset & Mental Resilience
    - **Morning Priming:** Meditation, visualisation, or gratitude to set a strong

mental state.

- **Journalling or Reflection:** Writing down goals, wins, and lessons daily.
- **Continuous Learning:** Reading, listening to podcasts, or studying successful people.

2. Physical Health & Energy

- **Exercise & Movement:** A non-negotiable habit for peak energy levels.
- **Nutrition & Hydration:** Fuelling the body for clarity, not just comfort.
- **Sleep & Recovery:** The secret weapon of high performers.

3. Business & Productivity Habits

- **Time Blocking:** Planning the day for deep, focused work.
- **Daily 'MIT' (Most Important Task):** Prioritising one major win each day.
- **No Distraction Rule:** Managing emails, social media, and calls in set blocks of time.

4. Relationships & Influence
    - **Intentional Networking:** Building meaningful connections daily.
    - **Team Leadership & Delegation:** Checking in with key people.
    - **Family & Personal Time:** Scheduling quality moments with loved ones.

5. Wealth & Financial Growth
    - **Daily Financial Awareness:** Tracking income, expenses, and investments.
    - **Wealth-Building Habits:** Studying markets, improving business cash flow, and focusing on wealth creation and protection both inside and outside the business. Reviewing long, mid, and short-term goals.
    - **Giving Back & Abundance Mindset:** Practicing generosity.

The 30-Day Habit Challenge

"Success is not about luck, talent, or intelligence. It's about the habits you execute daily. What you do every day will define who you become." *Tom Luttrell*

Now, it's time for action. I challenge you to reshape your life over the next 90 days. I promise that if you commit, your life will change in the most positive way.

I won't share all my habits, as some may not be relevant to you, but I do want to share how I set my day up for success:

- 5:00 AM: Wake up (often I'm awake earlier)
- 5:00 - 5:45 AM: Review goals, meditate, check my diary, and send key emails. This is my "me time" to get focused and feel organised. (And yes, coffee!)
- 5:45 - 6:00 AM: Drive to the gym while listening to an audiobook or my gym music and usually eating bananas.
- 6:00 - 7:00 AM: Gym workout—a

program designed specifically for my body, strength, and conditioning. The plan varies daily, which I enjoy. I have set goals and track them.

- 7:00 - 7:15 AM: Ice bath, sauna, cold shower, then get ready for the day.
- 8:00 AM: Breakfast and work session in the business lounge. First, I confirm all my appointments and calls for the day. I am set up for success and always feel good.

Your Challenge

Write down five new habits that you will implement every day for 90 days. Keep a journal to track your progress. Be honest with yourself—no cheating!

Stick with it, and I promise—you'll see the difference.

Good luck!

Strategy 32

Never Trust A Wolf in Sheep's Clothing

"The snake that cannot shed its skin must perish." - Friedrich Nietzsche

No matter what business you run or the sector you are in, at some stage, someone is going try to take advantage of you which normally means you are parting with money; you are getting ripped off.

Sometimes the con will be major, and other times the con will be far more subtle. A good example of something subtle is when you place an order for goods and the company you think you have bought the goods from never sends the goods, you chase, get frustrated, and ask for a refund but you have no success. Eventually, you find out the company has closed for business and the owners have disappeared. You with lots of others have been involved in a con. This is very common.

The trick with a con is to spot it coming. From my own experience, I learnt the hard way. At the time it was a sizeable con, and it hurt. Mostly, I was embarrassed and angry with myself BUT it has saved me many times since from others trying to do the same. Today, I can spot a con a mile off.

Here is my rule: The more you really need something the less you spot the red flags. Get really good at spotting red flags.

Let me tell you the story of the snakeoil salesman, **Jeff Dias.**

After the 2008 crash without us and most other people around the world knowing the world was pretty much bankrupt, it was a terrible time. As a business, we were scrambling like mad to find new money to prop our business up. At that time, everything we owned was at risk, we had personal guarantees against all of our assets. In short, if we did not find new money, we would lose everything, and that included most of our investors' funds also. The stakes were very high in 2009.

Out of the blue, a friend messaged me and said, "Tom I have met this guy and he has direct access to a line of credit out of the US. His name is Jeff and he wants you to call him."

Now, by 2009 I had spent 13 years as a corporate Financial Adviser and I had built a very successful property development business. I tell you this not to brag but to tell you I had been around the block and I thought I was good at reading people.

Jeff spoke the right property development language, he was organised, easy to like, slick, and coincidentally had his offices near my home in Buckinghamshire, really nice offices in a converted barn. I liked him instantly.

He and I had a series of meetings over a 2–3-week period. To cut a long story short, after 4 weeks I received a proposal from him. He said that he had spoken to his US funders and they had agreed in principle to provide a facility to us of $80m. Jeff produced a series of documents including a term sheet.

$80m solved all of our problems and gave us enough runway so that we would not need to go back for more money. I was both delighted and massively relieved.

The problem was I was desperate and didn't spot the red flags!

At the time. the company's cash flow was destroyed we were literally running on fumes. I spent the weekend reviewing the term sheet and all of the accompanying documents Jeff had produced, everything seemed to be in order. For the first time in 6 years, I did not send the documents to our lawyer Mayor Browne (then one of the top 10 law firms in the world). Why? We couldn't afford the fees and I felt experienced enough to review the documents myself. I had been working with our lawyer Andrew at MB for 6 years and had learnt a lot about legal contracts and structuring property deals.

Here are the first red flags, I liked Jeff but actually, I didn't know him and I did not check him out properly. I/we were desperate for the funds, I wanted to believe he had access to the money and he would get it for us.

Next, Jeff sent me a further note on the following Monday which basically said that he was really pleased that I was happy in principle with his proposal. He also said that there was a discounted commitment fee which needed to be paid upfront of Euro 120k. Red flag number 3. I was shocked because a commitment fee had not been mentioned. I went back to Jeff to ask him why the fee had not been mentioned and he said that he had mentioned there would be a fee at our first meeting. He didn't but I wanted to keep the process moving, we needed the $80m.

Jeff explained that the fee would be split between his firm, the US funders, and 2 sets of US lawyers. When I broke down who was getting what, it seemed reasonable for an $80m facility. I wasn't happy and we didn't have 120k. Also, I had told my business partner and our Chairman I had agreed to the funds in principle and now I had to tell them we had to find a further Euro 120k.

We had a board meeting where I presented the term sheet and the accompanying documents. I also told them there was a commitment fee of Euro 120k. After about an hour of kicking the deal around, Jeff turned up, I had invited him to come and meet the guys. He did, presented well, and convinced all 3 of us that he had his fingers on the funds. After he left, we agreed by hook or by crook we needed to find the commitment fees and we did. Red flag number 4!

We paid the money across and that was the worst financial mistake I have ever made. Nine months after we paid the funds, we were still not in funds. Jeff came up with one plausible excuse after another. Red flag number 5. Remember what I said earlier when you are desperate you don't see the flags.

Then one day in November, Jeff sent some new documents confirming that there would be a transfer on the 10th of December, at last! Jeff was finally delivering. I cannot tell you how relieved I was. I told the board and we were all very happy and looking forward to the 10th. We tied up some legal contracts with Jeff`s firm. Jeff was to receive the funds and then pay us. I didn't have a problem with this. Red flag number 6.

By now you know the story, the money didn't arrive on the 10th. Jeff made another excuse and said the money would arrive between Christmas and New Year. Red flag 7. I cannot remember what day I lost the plot in early January but I did. I finally realised Jeff was a con man and full of shit. I finally found out what I didn't want to know.

Jeff was ripping people off. Promising funds when developers like us were desperate for money, charging large upfront fees. A good con. I can remember being physically sick for days. I knew our business was dead and our investors would lose their money, we would lose everything also. It was the beginning of the end.

God only knows how many other people he ripped off. Beware of a wolf in sheep's clothing.

The moral of the Jeff story? Don't just look at what is nice and shiny on the surface; look underneath and dig deep. Don't trust someone because you think you like them. Do your DD. If it's a large transaction, always use your lawyer. Con men are normally scared of lawyers; most will back out of the con.

Since the Jeff con, I have had others try to rip me off 3 times. The worst was in 2022 so not long ago (Feb 4th, 2025 today).

I got introduced to a guy called Robert. He was referred to me by a successful financial adviser I knew at the time. I was told that Robert specialised in raising equity for property developers. This got my interest because it's something I have also done for many years. Property developers often need to access other people's money to get their deals done. There are lots of property developers in the UK so there is always a need for money which keeps the world spinning.

Robert and I shared a few emails and it seemed we might be able to collaborate on some deals. I had access to UK money and Robert told me that he had access to a significant amount of Euro money, Robert is Dutch.

We agreed to have a call. We spoke the following week for about an hour and the call went very well, with no red flags. Robert spoke the right language so I knew he had experience, he explained what types of deals he had funded in the past.

He told me about his sources for accessing equity. He also described a couple of deals he had on his desk, one of which was for a UK developer. I liked the deal and I knew if the deal was as Robert described I could get it funded. We agreed to meet in London and focus on this one deal first.

When we met, I was firstly impressed with Robert's dress and how pleasant he was. Not overdressed but smart. Remember, never trust a wolf in sheep's clothing!

We discussed the deal at length, I needed to understand everything about the deal including what was in it for me. How much equity did the guy need and how much debt and construction finance did he also need? Debt finance for property deals comes from financial institutions like banks and specialist funding houses. We spent a few hours together.

I told Robert I would speak to some of my relationships about investing and get back to him. This is when the red flags started going up!

1. Robert set a call up with me and his client. The developer was very experienced, a good guy, and knew his stuff. He told me he had paid Robert £5k as a commitment fee. I was

super surprised because Robert had not mentioned it. Anyway, I brushed over it because I needed to speak to Robert, my job was to find the equity not deal directly with Robert's client but I am now very concerned, not about the fee because it could be justified but why he had not told me!

2. The same day, Robert sent me 3 other deals. My immediate reaction was, why are you sending me more deals when we have agreed we would get one deal done first before working on anything else? Also, I thought to myself, "If you have all the Euro money at your fingertips why are you sending me all these other deals?" Another big red flag went up

I set a call up with Robert the next day. My gut is telling me there is a problem. On the call, I am pleasant and ask further questions about the deal. Toward the end of the call, I ask Robert about the £5k. He tells me that he charges every client £5k upfront and that going forward, he and I would split this fee. This is a problem for me because the maximum commitment fee I ever charge is £1500 and I only normally charge this if the deal is a little complicated.

I then asked him about the other deals he had sent and I asked him has he charged each of the developers £5k. He confirms he has and in that moment, 5 red flags go up and I immediately know what he is doing.

It's a kind of Ponzi scheme, he is charging developers 5k upfront and promising them money, only he does not have access to Euro money, it's bullshit.

He then hopes to plug into someone like me who will get the funding he needs and he moves on to the next victim. This works if he can find people like me. What he was actually doing at the time was taking circa £25k in fees, if any of the developers got really pissed off with him for not delivering the funds, he would repay 50% of the £5k they had paid him.

This money would come from his next victim. He would apologise to the developer and come up with a good excuse for why he couldn't get the money they needed. He would tell them as a gesture of good faith he would be returning 50% of the fee that they had paid him. A good con.

Anyway, I was furious with him (Jeff Dias very much on my mind). It's people like Robert that give the industry a bad name. I didn't tell him I was furious or I knew the con. By now he thinks we are best buddies.

I set another call up with him. On the call, I purposely go out of my way to be super friendly, and let him know that I am excited about working with him and how much money we can make. The call goes really well. Toward the end of the call, I set the trap. I ask him about the 5k fees and I suggest to him it's a great way to solve cash flow problems. I tell him we could get 20 developers to pay us £5k each even though we may not be able to find the money that each of them needs. I tell him that they would never know that we do not think their project is fundable but as they would be desperate, they would still pay the 5k. Now I am speaking Robert's language and he loves it, he opens up about other ways we could get money from developers, and he now thinks he and I are partners in crime.

The next day, I am ready, I set up another call. I let him have it with both barrels. I tell him to admit what he has done and if he does, I won't take things further but I will not work with him anymore. I tell him if he does not admit it, I will take it further. Eventually, he spills the beans and admits everything and more. It was worse than I thought. Little did he know that I had already reported him to Action Fraud. AC is connected to the fraud team within the Police.

I rang the developer who I had spoken to only a few days earlier and told him that Robert had conned him out of £5k and that he would not be getting the funds he needed from Robert. I apologised that I was nearly involved and I wished I could help him but I needed to distance myself from Robert.

I never heard from Robert again and I have no clue whether the developer got his money back.

The moral of this story? There are plenty of Roberts out there so get really good at spotting red flags.

Strategy 33

The Power of High-Performance Teams with a Common Goal

"Individual commitment to a group effort—that is what makes a team work, a company work, a society work, a civilisation work." - Vince Lombardi

Over the past 30 years, I've had the privilege of working alongside some truly exceptional talent. I've also had the opportunity to build two outstanding teams across two distinct sectors.

I'm not sharing this to boast but to emphasise the experience I've gained from training thousands of salespeople in financial services and property.

The impact of individuals uniting with a shared purpose to form a high-performing team is extraordinary.

If your business relies on people—especially salespeople—I strongly recommend implementing the strategy outlined in this section. It can transform how your team operates and achieves success.

Firstly, what are the characteristics of high-performance teams? What do members share in common?

1. Clear Goals and Vision: They have a shared purpose, with every team member understanding how their role contributes to overarching goals.

2. Strong Leadership: Effective leaders inspire, provide direction, and empower team members to perform at their best.

3. Open Communication: Team members share ideas freely, actively listen to one another, and provide constructive feedback.

4. Diverse Skillsets: They leverage the unique strengths, experiences, and perspectives of each team member.

5. Mutual Trust and Respect: There's a strong sense of psychological safety where individuals feel valued and supported.

6. Adaptability and Resilience: They respond quickly to challenges, embrace change, and maintain high morale under pressure.

7. Accountability: Each team member takes responsibility for their tasks and holds others accountable for shared goals.

8. Continuous Learning: High-performing teams seek growth, invest in training, and prioritise innovation.

9. Collaborative Mindset: Teamwork is a priority, with individuals putting the team's success above personal interests.

10. Focus on Results: They stay outcome-driven, ensuring that efforts align with achieving measurable success.

11. Empowerment and Autonomy: Members feel empowered to make decisions and take ownership of their tasks without constant supervision.

12. Emotional Intelligence: Team members show empathy, manage emotions effectively, and navigate interpersonal dynamics with maturity.

13. Alignment of Values: Shared values and a unified culture ensure team cohesion and reduce internal conflicts.

14. Efficient Conflict Resolution: Disagreements are addressed constructively, with a focus on finding solutions rather than assigning blame.

15. Role Clarity: Every member knows their responsibilities, reducing confusion and overlap.

16. Data-Driven Decision-Making: Decisions are guided by evidence, metrics, and feedback, ensuring smarter strategies and outcomes.

17. Celebration of Success: Wins, both big and small are celebrated.

18. Proactive Problem Solving: High-performance teams anticipate challenges and address them before they escalate.

19. Strong Work Ethic: Team members are committed, disciplined, and consistently give their best.

20. Positive Attitude: Optimism and enthusiasm permeate the team, fostering a can-do environment.

21. Effective Time Management: They prioritise tasks efficiently, meet deadlines, and avoid burnout.

22. Focus on Well-Being: Teams prioritise physical and mental health, understanding its impact on performance.

23. Commitment to Inclusion: Diverse perspectives are actively sought and valued, creating an inclusive environment.

24. Alignment with Organisational Goals: They understand how their work fits into the broader organisational strategy and stay aligned with it.

25. Agility in Decision-Making: Quick, thoughtful decision-making allows them to maintain momentum and adjust to new information.

26. High Levels of Engagement: Team members are highly motivated, emotionally invested, and enthusiastic about their roles.

27. Structured Processes: Clear workflows, defined protocols, and efficient systems ensure smooth operations.

28. Access to Resources: They are equipped with the tools, technology, and support they need to excel.

29. Innovation and Creativity: Encouraging experimentation and out-of-the-box thinking drives breakthroughs and problem-solving.

30. Resilience in Crisis: They stay composed, collaborate effectively, and maintain performance under pressure or during setbacks.

31. Commitment to Feedback Loops: Regular feedback cycles help refine performance and strengthen team dynamics.

32. Respect for Boundaries: Teams respect personal time and boundaries, fostering sustainable performance.

From experience, I can tell you that a group of highly motivated people with a common goal is the rocket fuel that will ensure you hit your targets and achieve your goals.

Here are my top 10 characteristics of high-performance individuals:

1. Clear Purpose and Vision

- They have a clear sense of purpose and long-term goals, which drives their actions.
- Example: A business owner who visualises scaling their company globally and aligns daily tasks with that vision.

2. Discipline and Consistency

- They show up every day, maintaining

habits and routines that support their growth.

- Example: Following a strict morning routine that includes exercise, reflection, and goal-setting.

3. Resilience and Adaptability

- They bounce back quickly from setbacks and adapt to new challenges with a positive mindset.
- Example: Pivoting business strategies when market conditions change unexpectedly.

4. Growth Mindset

- They constantly seek to learn and improve, seeing challenges as opportunities to grow.
- Example: Investing in courses or coaching to refine their leadership skills.

5. Focus and Prioritisation

- They can filter distractions and focus on the most impactful tasks.
- Example: Using the 80/20 rule to concentrate on tasks that drive 80% of results.

6. **Emotional Intelligence**
    - They manage their emotions well, build strong relationships, and communicate effectively.
    - Example: Handling team conflicts calmly and empathetically to find a resolution.
7. **Self-Motivation**
    - They don't rely on external factors for motivation; they are internally driven to achieve.
    - Example: Setting personal benchmarks to measure progress instead of waiting for validation.
8. **Health and Energy Management**
    - They prioritise physical and mental well-being to sustain high energy levels.
    - Example: Regular exercise, healthy eating, mindfulness practices, and quality sleep.
9. **Strong Work Ethic**
    - They are willing to put in the effort and go the extra mile to achieve excellence.
    - Example: Preparing thoroughly for a presentation, ensuring every detail is polished.

10. Strategic Risk-Taking

- They are not afraid to step out of their comfort zone and take calculated risks.
- Example: Launching a new product line after careful market research, despite potential challenges.

Strategy

Our goal when we built our financial services company was to build a company that was worth £1bn. That is probably £2bn in today's money. It was a big exciting goal.

What actually happened was a lot of change at the board level before we got to hit our goal. That being said, we did get to circa £500m in today's money which was still a massive achievement.

David and Stuart came up with a strategy that the company's divisional directors would meet once a month every month. We did this for 4 plus years. These meetings were held around the UK to make it fair for everyone on the team. The days were all about strategy, results, deliverables, and new projects. We had a laser focus on our main goal and we delivered.

If you have a team and you are able, take them off-site once a month and motivate, inspire, and drive them. Make sure they have a big goal and there is a massive reward when you all get there. You will be amazed where you will end up, trust me and go for it.

I often think about those days. We started with just 4 of us and ended up with 2300 people and 81 offices around the world. Amazing! Would we have got as far as we did without those meetings? **No, I am sure we would not have.** Would we have got more or less done without the meetings? **Less of course.**

Would the company have been worth more or less without the meetings? **Less.**

Would we have recruited more or less people? **Less.**

Here is the biggest benefit of those meetings, team bonding, camoradory, and lifelong friendships: Our ability to collectively focus on one big goal.

Action Point: Strengthen Team Connection & Performance

Step 1: Evaluate Your Current Team Engagement

Assess how often and in what format you are meeting with your team. Are your meetings productive? Do they foster collaboration, motivation, and alignment with business goals?

Step 2: Implement Regular, High-Impact Team Meetings

Face-to-face meetings are vital for **team bonding, communication, recognition, and motivation.** Create a structured plan for meetings that ensure they are **engaging, purposeful, and energising.**

Step 3: Foster a Culture of Open Communication & Recognition

Encourage transparency, active participation, and two-way feedback. Use meetings to **recognise achievements, address challenges, and inspire your team.**

Step 4: Create an Actionable Meeting Plan

Design a **new meeting strategy** that includes **clear objectives, an engaging format, and follow-up actions** to ensure every session adds value. Balance **structured meetings with informal team interactions** to strengthen relationships.

By optimising your team meetings, you will **enhance collaboration, boost morale, and create a high-performance work culture.**

Get Ready, There Will be a Storm

Strategy 34

The Dark Days

"Rock bottom became the solid foundation on which I rebuilt my life." - J.K. Rowling

In 2011, I was declared bankrupt. The fallout from 2008 had finally caught up with us. Everything we had leveraged was lost, leaving me with nothing but the proverbial "shirt on my back."

Strangely, it wasn't my personal losses that hurt the most—it was the loss of our investors' money. I was devastated. To this day, I reflect on that pain. While no one foresaw the crash, a few in the US understood what was happening behind closed doors with the banks. It was financial Armageddon, and despite our best efforts, we couldn't escape its grip.

I remember the overwhelming wave of emotions—shock, embarrassment, guilt. These feelings lingered for a long time and were difficult to shake. Professionally, I had worked for over 17 years by then, and now I had lost everything.

Emotionally, I was shattered. For a long time, I turned to drinking, numbing the pain and spiralling deeper into self-pity. But if there's one thing I've learnt through this painful experience, it's that numbing the pain—whether through alcohol, drugs, or other means—only makes things worse, often tenfold.

While it's easier said than done, what you need most in these moments is a clear head, even when you feel like you're on your knees.

If you have done it before you can do it again, no matter how bad it feels.

If you're struggling today, please don't hesitate to reach out to me. My contact details are at the back of this book. I'll do my best to help you cope with whatever challenges you're facing.

There's also plenty of support available, so take the first step and reach out.

Get Ready, There Will be a Storm

Strategy 35

Add Trevor to Your Bowling Team

"A rising tide lifts all boats." - John F. Kennedy

A few years ago, I had a solid team. The men and women were professional, focused, and consistently good at hitting their targets. Things were running smoothly, and I felt confident in our collective performance.

Then, out of the blue, a friend called and mentioned someone he knew from the local Ten Pin Bowling club—a guy named Jeff. According to my friend, Jeff had the potential to excel in our environment. He'd already spoken to Jeff, who was interested in a chat with me. We met, and my friend was absolutely right: Jeff was perfect for the team.

Jeff, in his early 30s, was immaculately dressed, exuded confidence, spoke exceptionally well, and had a spark that was hard to ignore. When he joined us, it didn't take long for him to shine.

The interesting thing? I already had a high-performing team, but Jeff's arrival changed the dynamics entirely. Overnight, he raised the bar. Suddenly, my top performers were no longer at the top—Jeff had claimed that spot. He was the first one in the office and the last to leave. When he wasn't working, he was at the gym, keeping himself physically and mentally sharp. He was the dream recruit and, as it turned out, a phenomenal bowler too!

Salespeople are naturally competitive, and Jeff's energy and performance put everyone under pressure. It was exhilarating to watch as my team began breaking their own records, striving to keep up with him.

The takeaway? Always keep an eye out for the Jeffs of the world—the ones with the spark, the drive, and the determination to raise the bar. Adding someone like that to your team can instantly elevate performance across the board. Find them, hire them, and let the competition work its magic.

Get Ready, There Will be a Storm

Strategy 36

Cybersecurity and Hackers: The Invisible Enemy Why Cybersecurity is No Longer Optional

"If you spend more on coffee than on IT security, you will be hacked. What's more, you deserve to be hacked." – Richard Clarke

Most businesses focus on financial security but overlook digital security—until they get hacked. Cybercrime is now one of the biggest **financial threats** to businesses, costing companies **billions every year**.

A few years ago, my LinkedIn account got hacked. Why? Simple really and it's a mistake so many business owners make.

An old business associate managed to access my password. He then systematically copied and even moved some of my 23,000 contacts. I only found out what he was doing because I got a message from a guy in Africa about a gold deal. Confused, I tried to get to the bottom of the problem, eventually I asked the chap who he thought he was dealing with and he gave me the name of the ex-business colleague. Soon after I discovered what was happening and I spoke with LinkedIn and they transferred all of my contacts to a new account. It was an eye-opener and taught me a valuable lesson.

Here's the hard truth: Small businesses are the most **targeted** because hackers know they often lack strong cybersecurity measures. If your systems are **breached**, your **data, customers, reputation, and money** are at risk.

The 3 Biggest Cybersecurity Threats to Business Owners

1. **Phishing Attacks**
    - Fake emails that **look legitimate** (pretending to be your bank, suppliers, or even employees).
    - Hackers **trick you into clicking links or giving login details**.
    - **Example:** You get an email from "PayPal" saying your account is locked—when you click the link, hackers steal your credentials.
2. **Ransomware Attacks**
    - Hackers **lock your data** and demand **a ransom** to restore access.
    - Small businesses are prime targets because they **can't afford downtime**.
    - **Example:** I know of a UK

businessman who paid £20,000 to regain access to his customer database. An old business acquaintance was to blame in the end.

3. **Weak Passwords & Insider Threats**
   - 80% of data breaches happen because of **weak or stolen passwords**.
   - **Example:** Employees using "password123" or **sharing passwords across multiple accounts** can lead to breaches.
   - Insider threats (disgruntled employees) can also **sell company data** to hackers.

The 5-Step Cybersecurity Protection Plan for Business Owners

Business owners **don't need to be tech experts**, but they **must take basic precautions**. Here's what you **must** do to **protect your business**:

1. **Use Strong, Unique Passwords & Multi-Factor Authentication (MFA)**

- **Do NOT reuse passwords** across accounts. Use **password managers** like 1Password or LastPass.
- Turn on **Multi-Factor Authentication (MFA)** (e.g., a code sent to your phone when logging in).
- Require **employees to follow strict password policies**.

2. Train Employees to Recognise Cyber Threats

- **Teach your team about phishing emails**—train them to **never click** suspicious links.
- Run **fake phishing tests** to see if employees are vulnerable.
- Establish **a security policy**—what to do when a suspicious email or activity is detected.

3. Secure Your Business Devices & Networks

- Always update **software & systems**—hackers exploit outdated software.
- Use **firewalls & antivirus software** on all company devices.

- Encrypt sensitive data & **use VPNs** for remote work.

4. **Protect Customer & Financial Data**
   - Store sensitive business & customer data **in secure, encrypted cloud services**.
   - Restrict **who has access** – employees should only access data **they need**.
   - Regularly **backup all data** to a secure **offline location** (so hackers can't delete everything).
5. **Have an Emergency Cybersecurity Plan**
   - What if you get hacked? Have **a crisis plan** ready.
   - **Who do you call?** Cybersecurity expert, IT provider, or legal team?
   - **Can you recover quickly?** If ransomware hits, do you have backups?

A Real-World Business Cybersecurity Case Study

Many business owners ignore cybersecurity **until disaster strikes**. Here's a powerful example:

Case Study: How a Small Business Lost £50,000 Overnight

A small London-based eCommerce store received an email from **"their bank"** asking them to confirm their login details due to "suspicious activity." The email looked real, so the business owner **entered their credentials**.

What happened next?

- Hackers **gained access** to their business bank account and transferred **£50,000 out** within hours.
- The bank **refused to refund the money** because it was an **authorised transaction** (even though it was fraud).
- Their business **almost collapsed** overnight. Luckily in the end the funds were returned.

Lesson learnt:

- The business now uses **MFA, strict access controls, and phishing training**.

Closing Challenge for Business Owners

Cybersecurity is not just for big corporations – it's for EVERY business.

Implement **at least 3 cybersecurity steps** from this chapter in the next **7 days**.

Test your team: **Send a fake phishing email** – see if they recognise the scam.

Review your **password policies** and set up **Multi-Factor Authentication** today.

Don't wait for a cyberattack to take cybersecurity seriously. Protect your business NOW.

Strategy 37

The Numbers Don't Lie—Many Property Development Deals Don't Add Up

"In real estate, you make your money when you buy, not when you sell." - Warren Buffett

My brother John has been helping property developers secure funding for over 20 years. To date, he has raised well over £1 billion for various projects.

Time and again, he meets developers—some seasoned, some new—who have an exciting project and are looking for acquisition and construction finance. At first glance, these deals often look promising. You estimate acquisition costs, construction expenses, and potential profits, and it's easy to get caught up in the excitement of the numbers.

But here's the challenge: many developers, regardless of experience, sometimes overlook critical costs or underestimate key factors.

These oversights can make or break a project. What initially seems like a lucrative opportunity can quickly turn into a financial disaster.

To ensure your property development deals are viable, you need to be meticulous in evaluating every aspect of the project. Here's a comprehensive list of factors to consider:

1. **Acquisition Costs**: The purchase price of the land or property, including stamp duty, legal fees, and associated taxes.
2. **Construction Costs:** All building-related expenses, from materials to labour.
3. **Financing Costs:** Interest payments, arrangement fees, and any associated borrowing costs.
4. **Professional Fees:** Payments to architects, engineers, surveyors, and planners.
5. **Legal Fees:** Conveyancing, contracts, and additional legal requirements.
6. **Insurance:** Coverage during construction and beyond.
7. **Affordable Housing Contributions:** Many councils require a percentage of the development to be allocated for affordable housing. Failing to account for this can erode profits or derail financing approval.
8. **Community Infrastructure Levy (CIL)**: Local authorities may impose a CIL charge, which can add significant costs depending on the scale and location of the project.

9. Market Conditions: Current demand, future trends, and potential risks.
10. Sales Costs: Marketing, estate agents' fees, and other costs tied to selling the finished property.
11. Contingency Fund: An allowance for unexpected expenses or delays. A good rule of thumb is at least 10% of total costs.
12. Profit Margin: The realistic return after all costs – including regulatory requirements – are accounted for.

If you're embarking on a new project and want a second pair of eyes or expert advice, don't hesitate to reach out to John. He doesn't charge upfront fees and would be delighted to support you. You can email him at john@appellacommercialfinance.co.uk.

Remember: The key to successful property development is not just finding the right project but ensuring every detail is accounted for. Let John help you avoid the pitfalls and set yourself up for success.

Strategy 38

Induction Day—Make Day One Amazing

"Take care of your employees, and they will take care of your business." - Richard Branson

It always surprises me how often business owners underestimate the importance of a new recruit's first day.

Hiring the right person often requires significant effort—time spent sourcing, interviewing, and onboarding, not to mention potential recruitment fees if an agency is involved. That's why the first day isn't just another workday—it's a pivotal moment to set the tone for their future in your business.

Here's the step-by-step process I recommend to all my clients when they bring a new recruit on board:

1. **Be Super Prepared:** Plan out their first day and first week in detail. Provide them with a written schedule so they know exactly what to expect.
2. **A Warm Welcome:** Invite them in early—before the rest of the team arrives—for coffee or tea and a croissant. Take this time to express how excited you are to have them join. Leave a card on their desk welcoming them to the office, and sign it.

3. **Open the Floor:** Ask them what questions they have. What are they unsure about? What are they most excited about?
4. **Address Feelings:** Ask if they're feeling nervous and discuss those feelings openly.
5. **Motivate Them:** Share your vision for the business and how they'll play a role in achieving it.
6. **Paint Their Future:** Outline the growth and opportunities you see for them within the company.
7. **Personal Introductions:** Introduce them to each team member individually, making them feel part of the group.
8. **Explain the Basics:** Clarify break times, workplace etiquette, and anything else they might wonder about.
9. **Assign a Buddy:** Pair them with a trusted team member who loves the business. Make it clear the buddy is there to provide support.
10. **End-of-Day Check-In:** Have a one-on-one at the end of the day to ask how things went and address any concerns.
11. **Day 2 Kick-Off:** Spend ten minutes with

them in the morning to see how they're feeling.

12. **Buddy Feedback:** Check in with the buddy to see how the new recruit is settling in.

13. **End-of-Week Review:** Schedule a 30-minute one-on-one on their first Friday to review their experience and provide feedback.

Why This Works

By following this process, you'll achieve one of two outcomes:

1. **A Happy Recruit:** They'll feel welcomed, valued, and excited to stay because you've demonstrated that you care about their success.
2. **A Quick Resolution:** If they're not the right fit, you'll identify it early. Recruitment isn't just about hiring; it's about finding the right match for your team and your vision. It's better to address potential mismatches sooner rather than later.

Remember, the goal of this process is to ensure a strong start and to discover quickly whether you and the new recruit are a good fit. If failure is inevitable, fail fast – whether it's a person or a project. This will save time, money, and morale in the long run.

Action point: Put in writing a new induction plan. Share this plan with everyone in your team responsible for recruitment and inducting new people. Then measure it!! Check that it is being implemented.

Get Ready, There Will be a Storm

Strategy 39

Email Marketing: Play the Long Game

"People don't buy when you want to sell. They buy when they are ready." - Jeffrey Gitomer

Over the years, I've been involved in countless email campaigns, both for clients and my own businesses. Some campaigns were highly successful, while others taught valuable lessons.

The key takeaway? Email marketing works if you have a solid plan and the patience to play the long game. Many business owners I meet expect immediate results, but that's unrealistic unless you strike it incredibly lucky.

Experts say it now takes **12 touchpoints** for a cold lead to trust you enough to buy—that's a lot!

With that in mind, here are some essential strategies for successful email marketing:

1. Start with Quality Data

Be GDPR-Compliant: If you don't already have a list, you can either buy GDPR-compliant data or, better yet, collaborate with complementary businesses. Partner with them to market your product or service to their database, using a commission or fee-sharing model.

2. Use the Right Email Platform

Invest in a robust email marketing platform. I've tried many, but **Smartlead.ai** stands out by a mile today. It's AI-driven, user-friendly, and highly effective at avoiding spam filters. Plus, it provides excellent insights (MI) and is more affordable than most platforms. We are clients. Contact them here https://smartlead.ai?via=tom-luttrell

3. Warm Up Cold Contacts

Don't rush to sell. Start by creating a series of messages to send over 3 months. The frequency is up to you—once a week or every few days—but don't overwhelm your audience.

Focus on **educating and engaging**: Share valuable industry insights, economic updates, or relevant statistics. Offer freebies like e-books, audits, free trials, or even one-on-one sessions.

Deadlines work wonders—use real ones, like a tax break deadline, to create urgency.

4. Monitor and Optimise Your Campaigns
Analyse the insights (MI) from your platform to see what works and what doesn't.

5. Test and Refine Subject Lines
A/B test subject lines to maximise open rates. Personalisation is key—emails with the recipient's first name in the subject line perform better. What would you prefer?
Example:

- *Act today before you lose this tax break*
- *John, act today before you lose this tax break*

6. Stay On-Brand
Use your logo and brand colours in your email designs to reinforce your identity.

7. Include a Clear Call to Action
Always guide the reader to their next step, whether it's looking out for your next email, clicking a link to a landing page, or scheduling a meeting.

8. Simplify Scheduling with Calendly

Calendly is a fantastic tool that allows recipients to book directly into your calendar. It's efficient and cost-effective.

Final Thought

Email marketing isn't about instant gratification—it's about building trust and delivering value over time. When done right, it can become one of your most powerful marketing channels.

Get Ready, There Will be a Storm

Strategy 40

Focus on What You Do Best, Leave the Rest

"Do what you do best and outsource the rest."
- Peter Drucker

If I had a pound or dollar for every business owner I've met over the past 30 years who tried to do it all themselves, I'd be incredibly wealthy.

Let me share a real-life example to illustrate why this approach doesn't work. If you find yourself nodding along, it's time to make a change – quickly!

Maria's Story

Maria is a brilliant conveyancing lawyer – how do I know? She's my lawyer and a trusted friend! With over 30 years of experience, Maria excels at what she does: she's meticulous, client-focused, and rarely makes mistakes. She's never had a PI claim, and nearly all her business comes from referrals or repeat clients – an undeniable mark of quality. mboulter@mblawyers.co.uk

But Maria has one major challenge: **she struggles to let go.**

She spends countless hours on administrative tasks she could delegate, robbing herself of the time to work directly with clients. I estimate Maria earns £250–£500 per hour when meeting clients, yet she insists on handling admin work that a skilled administrator could do for £15–£18 per hour.

It seems obvious, doesn't it? Maria should focus on her high-value work and leave the admin to someone else. Yet, like many business owners, she finds it hard to delegate.

Why Do Business Owners Struggle to Delegate?

Here are some common reasons:

1. Fear of Mistakes

Delegating important admin tasks feels risky. What if someone messes up? While this fear is valid, it's also counterproductive. Overstretching yourself increases the likelihood of making mistakes. The solution? Hire a competent, detail-oriented administrator you can trust.

2. Added Payroll Costs

Paying someone to handle admin work might seem like an unnecessary expense. But this thinking is short-sighted. Delegating frees up your time to focus on revenue-generating activities, ultimately increasing your income and improving your daily work satisfaction.

3. Time Needed to Train

Training a new team member can feel like a daunting task—it's true that initially, it may take more time. However, the right hire will quickly adapt to your processes and systems, and their efficiency will save you countless hours in the long run.

Finding the Right Fit

The key to successful delegation is finding the right person. Look for someone who:

- Is highly organised and has a strong track record.
- Listens and adapts to your needs.
- Gets along well with you and your team.

Once you've found the right person, use the **Induction Process** outlined earlier in this book to set them up for success.

Final Thought

Don't let fear or hesitation stop you from delegating. Focus on what you do best, and let a skilled team handle the rest. Your productivity, happiness, and bottom line will thank you!

Action Points: Mastering Delegation for Growth

Step 1: Identify Your High-Value Work

Make a list of tasks you handle daily and **categorise them** into two sections:

- High-impact work that only you can do (e.g., client meetings, strategic planning).
- Low-value tasks that someone else could handle (e.g., admin, invoicing, scheduling).

Step 2: Calculate the Cost of Doing It All

Ask yourself: **What is your hourly rate?** If you make £250 per hour but spend time on £15 tasks, you're losing money. This shift in perspective helps justify hiring support.

Step 3: Find & Hire the Right Support

Look for a **competent, detail-oriented assistant** who can take over non-core tasks. Focus on:

- Strong organisational skills.
- Ability to learn quickly and adapt to your workflow.
- Compatibility with your work style and team.

Step 4: Train & Trust the Process

Use the **Induction Process** outlined earlier to ensure a smooth handover. Start with **small, low-risk tasks**, then gradually **increase responsibility** as trust grows.

Step 5: Measure the Impact

Regularly assess whether delegation is **saving you time and increasing revenue**. If needed, refine your approach and optimise efficiency.

By focusing on what you do best and delegating the rest, you'll free up time, improve productivity, and scale your business with less stress.

Strategy 41

Know Your Story

"If you can't explain it simply, you don't understand it well enough." - Albert Einstein

It's astonishing how many business owners stumble when asked a simple question: *"What do you do?"* Instead of a clear, compelling answer, I often get something muddled and confusing.

Why does this happen? Usually, it's for one of these reasons:

1. **Fear of Public Speaking**: They're nervous and clam up in front of someone new.
2. **Lack of Preparation**: They haven't taken the time to refine their story.
3. **Underestimating its Importance**: They don't think having a clear story matters.

Why Your Story Matters

This book is filled with strategies to help you succeed, and having a polished, powerful story is one of the most crucial. Why?

1. You'll represent yourself and your business more effectively.
2. You'll set an example for your team, enabling them to share the company story with confidence.

As the leader, you may know your business inside out and instinctively present well. But your team? They need clear guidance, structure, and practice to deliver the story as effectively as you do.

The Power of a Well-Drilled Team

Every team member needs an elevator pitch—a concise, impactful version of the company story. And they need to be drilled on it regularly.

Here's a simple strategy I used: **Friday Morning Meetings.**

- **Timing**: These meetings were mandatory, and punctuality was non-negotiable. If someone was late, they couldn't join (plus they knew they would be in a 1-1 with me after the meeting!).
- **Purpose**: Fridays were an opportunity to thank the team, celebrate wins, share updates, and reinforce the company story.

- **Story Practice**: I'd select a team member to present the pitch in front of everyone. I often chose someone who was confident and polished to set the tone. Then, I'd call on a couple of juniors to do the same.

This process worked wonders. No one wanted to stand up unprepared, so they practiced like mad—especially in the early months. Over time, the entire team became sharp, confident, and consistent in delivering the story to new prospects.

Try This Strategy

Implementing regular storytelling practice in your team will:

1. Sharpen everyone's skills.
2. Build confidence.
3. Ensure your company's message is delivered consistently and effectively.

A well-rehearsed story can make the difference between winning or losing a new client. So, invest the time—it's worth it.

Strategy 42

Your Secret Wealth—Contacts and Connections

"The richest people in the world look for and build networks, everyone else looks for work."
- Robert Kiyosaki

I was chatting with my son, Oli, the other day about marketing and revenue generation. Oli runs a very niche marketing business, and like many business owners, he was laser-focused on generating more and more leads to drive subscriber growth. Normally, I'd agree with this strategy, but in Oli's case, it was creating problems.

In just 8 weeks, Oli had brought in over 4,000 new customers. That's an impressive achievement, but his sales team couldn't keep up. Instead of delivering great service to existing and new subscribers, they were stretched too thin—doing a mediocre job for everyone.

I explained this to Oli and suggested three immediate actions:

1. Stop Adding More Fuel to the Fire

The business was already overwhelmed with leads, and they were being wasted due to insufficient follow-up. I advised Oli to stop generating new leads temporarily and focus on properly serving the ones he already had.

2. Maximise the Value of Existing Subscribers

Instead of chasing new leads, Oli needed to focus on nurturing and maximising revenue from his current customer base. Upselling, cross-selling, and providing exceptional service to his existing subscribers would generate more revenue without adding strain.

3. Make Structural Improvements

We took a step back to evaluate the business holistically, identifying areas for improvement:

- **Recruitment and Training**: His team needed more people and better training to handle the growing customer base.
- **Systems and Processes**: Implementing more efficient workflows would ensure smoother operations.
- **Revenue Diversification**: Relying on a single revenue stream is risky. We

brainstormed additional income sources to safeguard the business against potential disruptions.

Oli embraced the changes, and they worked. His business is thriving, and revenue is up significantly. What he doesn't know yet is that I'll be pushing him for another gear change in 2025!

The Takeaway

If you're in a similar position, here's my advice:

- **Focus on What You Have**: Before generating more leads, ensure your existing customers are well-served and your operations can handle growth.
- **Train Your People**: Your team should be as skilled and confident as you are – if not better.
- **Review Your Processes**: Are your systems as efficient and effective as they could be?

- **Prepare for the Next Gear Change**: Growth is about continuous improvement. Always ask yourself: *What needs to change now to set me up for future success?*

Sometimes, scaling back and reassessing can be the most profitable decision you make.

Strategy 43

People's Most Dreaded Fear—Public Speaking

"You can speak well if your tongue can deliver the message of your heart."
- John Ford

If you're like most people, the thought of standing in front of an audience and delivering a speech is terrifying. Statistically, for every one person who's a natural public speaker, there are probably a hundred who are paralysed by the idea.

I know this because I was one of the 100. When I started out, public speaking felt alien. I'd get hot flushes, I tossed and turn the night before and got hardly any sleep, and spend days obsessively scripting. It was miserable.

Over time, I learnt that public speaking is a skill, not an innate talent. With practice and guidance, I not only overcame my fear but found joy in the process.

My journey showed me the transformative power of teaching this skill to others.

Why Invest in Public Speaking for Your Team?

If you commit to developing your team's public speaking abilities, you'll see incredible benefits:

1. **Improved Sales Performance**: Confidence is contagious. A team that communicates effectively will close more deals and make stronger impressions on clients.

2. **Team Bonding**: Public speaking is outside most people's comfort zones. Training sessions can be fun, filled with shared laughter and encouragement, and fostering camaraderie.

3. **Boosted Confidence**: Once your team conquers their fear of public speaking, their confidence will soar—not just in work, but in life.

A Word of Caution

For some, fear of public speaking isn't just nervousness; it's debilitating. For these individuals, throwing them into the deep end could crush their confidence. If you notice someone is genuinely terrified, give them one-on-one coaching before asking them to speak in front of a group.

How to Get Started

- **Hire a Trainer**: There are many skilled public speaking coaches who can work with your team. If budget permits, take the training off-site for a fresh and relaxed environment. Perhaps you are great at public speaking but you have never thought to actually train your team, now you can!
- **Create Opportunities**: During team meetings, give everyone a chance to present. Start with small, informal topics to ease them in.
- **Lead by Example**: If you're nervous about public speaking, share your story. Showing vulnerability can inspire others to face their fears.

A Legendary Test

Years after I first started public speaking, I faced one of the most challenging moments of my career.

Our company as mentioned earlier, was acquiring a massive life assurance salesforce—a 1000 plus people all at once. While most were excited to join us, a small group was deeply hostile.

We decided to host an event at the Cumberland Hotel in London, bringing 750 people together to share our vision and eliminate any miscommunication.

David our CEO asked me to present a key segment, persuading the group of the benefits of working independently with us. I agreed, driven by my own self-interest as a shareholder, but I was also nervous.

As the day unfolded, things got chaotic. Among the 750 attendees were a handful of dissenters who had decided to cause trouble. They stood up and heckled loudly throughout my presentation. Adding to the pressure, a film crew had a camera trained on me, and an artist sat in front sketching a caricature of me as I spoke.

What could have been a nightmare turned into one of my proudest moments. I delivered our message with confidence, despite the noise and distraction. How? Years of training, practice, and saying yes to every opportunity to speak had prepared me for that moment.

The Takeaway

Public speaking is a game-changer—for individuals, teams, and businesses. Invest in this skill for your people, and you'll see profound changes in their performance, confidence, and camaraderie.

Even if you or your team start out terrified, remember: with training and practice, you can transform fear into confidence. And one day, you might even find yourself standing in front of 750 people, hecklers and all, delivering a speech with ease.

Fear of Public Speaking: What the Stats Say

1. Glossophobia Affects 75% of People

According to the National Institute of Mental

Health (NIMH), about 75% of people experience some level of fear or anxiety when speaking in public. This can range from mild nervousness to full-blown panic.

2. Public Speaking Is a Bigger Fear Than Death for Some

A famous 1973 study by Bruskin-Goldring Research found that public speaking ranked as the number one fear among Americans—higher than the fear of death! This was popularised by comedian Jerry Seinfeld, who joked that at a funeral, most people would rather be in the coffin than giving the eulogy.

3. Only 10% Are 'Natural' Speakers

Studies suggest that only around 10% of people naturally enjoy and excel at public speaking, while another 10% experience extreme fear (glossophobia). The remaining 80% fall somewhere in between, experiencing varying levels of discomfort.

4. A Common Workplace Fear

A Chapman University survey in 2022 found

that fear of public speaking ranked among the top workplace anxieties, reinforcing that even professionals struggle with it.

Strategy 44

Your Secret Weapon—A Friendly Journalist

"If I was down to my last dollar, I would spend it on public relations." - Bill Gates

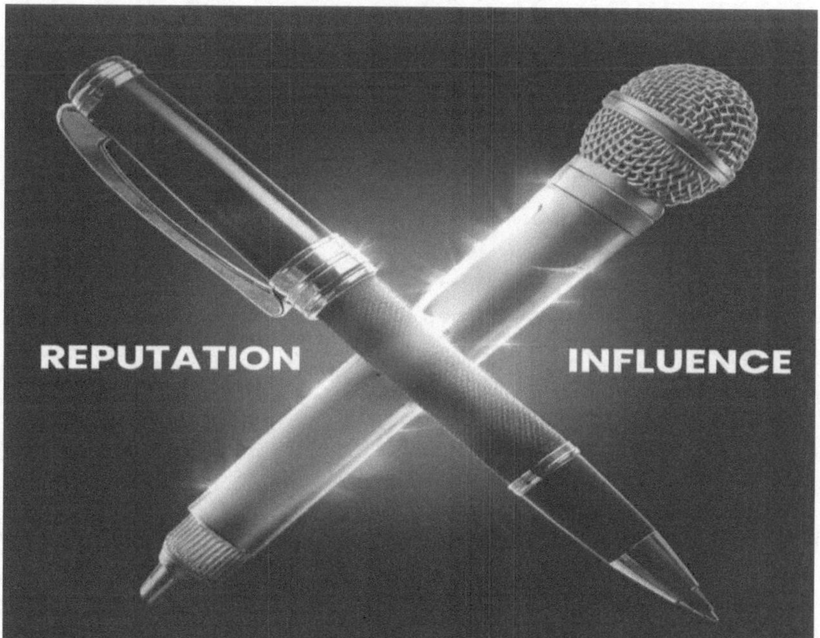

Few things are more powerful than third-party credibility—having a respected journalist write about you or your business. A well-placed article in a trusted publication can elevate your reputation, attract new clients, and open doors that no marketing campaign ever could.

The Power of Positive Press

Years ago, we had the good fortune of meeting Brian, a financial journalist who wrote for major publications, including national newspapers and the London Metro.

At first, Brian was sceptical about what we were building. And that's understandable—journalists are approached all the time by businesses desperate for exposure. Winning over a journalist isn't about selling—it's about building trust.

We invested months into the relationship. We invited Brian for lunch, introduced him to our team, and let him sit in on meetings. We didn't pitch him a story; we let him discover it himself.

It worked.

Over time, Brian wrote several glowing features about us. The impact was incredible:
1. Investors Paid Attention: Positive press gave us credibility, making it far easier to attract funding.
2. Clients Felt Reassured: When potential customers saw respected publications talking about us, it removed doubts and built instant trust.
3. Staff Morale Soared: Seeing our work featured in the press gave our team pride in what they were building.
4. Suppliers Took Us More Seriously: Strong media coverage gave us leverage in negotiations and strengthened key partnerships.

How to Build a Relationship with a Journalist
1. Do Your Research
Identify journalists who write about your

industry. Read their articles, understand their style, and figure out what interests them.

2. Make a Connection Before You Need Them
Follow them on LinkedIn, comment on their posts, and engage genuinely. Journalists receive hundreds of pitches a week – stand out by building rapport first.

3. Offer Real Value
Instead of pushing for coverage, offer insight. Share industry trends, unique data, or an expert opinion they can use in their reporting.

4. Make It Easy for Them
If a journalist does show interest, be ready with compelling, well-prepared information. Provide quotes, background, and supporting materials so they can write the story with minimal effort.

The Takeaway

A friendly journalist can be one of your most valuable assets. One great article can do more for your business than months of advertising.

Invest time in the relationship. Be helpful, be patient, and when the right moment comes, the press coverage they provide could be a game-changer for you.

Strategy 45

Balance

"Imagine life as a game in which you are juggling five balls... Work, family, health, friends, and spirit. Work is a rubber ball. If you drop it, it will bounce back. But the other four are made of glass." –
Brian Dyson (Former Coca-Cola CEO)

Balancing work and personal life is one of the hardest challenges for any entrepreneur or leader with significant responsibilities. Over the years, I've learnt this the hard way, experiencing both the highs of professional success and the lows of strained personal relationships.

While I don't have a magic pill to fix this, I do have some sound, hard-earned advice to share.

Understanding the Challenge

Building a business – or playing a major role in someone else's – is an all-consuming endeavour. The early years of a business require relentless effort:

- **Long hours**: Early mornings, late nights, and working weekends become the norm.
- **Tunnel vision**: Your mind is always on the business, leaving little space for family, friends, or even self-care.
- **Excitement and drive**: The thrill of

building something new can sometimes overshadow everything else.

Unfortunately, the people closest to you—your family, partner, and friends—don't always understand what it takes. They may see you as distant, unavailable, or even uncaring.

What You Can Do

1. **Communicate Clearly**
   - Explain what you're doing and why. Share your vision, goals, and the sacrifices required.
   - Help them see how they fit into the bigger picture.
   - Be transparent about the challenges and timelines.

Many years ago, I failed at this. My partner at the time felt ignored and unsupported. She saw my focus on the business as selfish, while I saw her frustrations as ungratefulness.

Looking back, the real issue was my lack of communication.

2. **Prioritise Quality Time**
    - It's not about spending endless hours together; it's about making the time you do have meaningful.
    - Plan activities that strengthen your connection – whether it's a weekend trip, a dinner out, or simply a walk together.

3. **Involve Them in the Journey**
    - Where appropriate, invite them to be part of your business story. This could be through updates, celebrations of milestones, or even occasional involvement in small tasks.

4. **Set Boundaries**
    - While you'll inevitably be working long hours, carve out specific times to unplug and focus on family or personal needs.
    - For example, create a no-work zone during meals or certain weekends.

5. **Recognise Their Contribution**
   - Your loved ones are making sacrifices too. Acknowledge their patience, support, and understanding.

A Personal Lesson

I'll never forget the Saturday my phone was ringing nonstop, and my partner voiced her frustration. My response? "When the phone stops ringing, *that's* when we have a problem!" Looking back, I can laugh at my lack of empathy and tact.

What I've come to realise is that balance doesn't mean equal time for work and home—it means ensuring that both aspects of your life are nurtured and valued.

The Takeaway

Balance isn't about perfection; it's about conscious effort. Building a business will test your relationships, but with clear communication, intentional time together, and mutual understanding, you can create harmony.

Your loved ones are part of your success story—treat them as such. A happy home is a foundation for long-term success. Seek it, nurture it, and don't let your professional ambitions overshadow what matters most.

Strategy 46

Burnout and Mental Health

"You can't pour from an empty cup. Take care of yourself first." - Tom Luttrell

Burnout is real, serious, and something most entrepreneurs or high-achievers face at some point. I know I have been there.

As I've said before, building a business requires *blood, sweat, and tears*. It's exhilarating and rewarding, but it's also relentless. Over time, the constant highs and lows, long hours, and unrelenting demands take their toll on everyone

Recognising Burnout

- Burnout often creeps up on you. You may start feeling:
- Constant fatigue, even after rest.
- Emotional detachment from your work or people around you.
- Irritability or a short temper.
- A lack of passion for what once fuelled you.
- Physical symptoms like headaches, muscle pain, or insomnia.

The truth is, even the most resilient among us have limits. It's important to recognise these signs and act before the damage becomes severe.

Knowing When It's Time for a Change

There comes a point when you just *know*—it's time to make a change. For some, this might mean:

1. **Selling the business** and stepping away entirely.
2. **Passing the reins** to a trusted team member while staying on as an advisor or board member.
3. **Scaling back** your involvement to focus on other aspects of life.

Whatever the decision, trust your instincts and listen to your body. Ignoring these signals can lead to prolonged burnout, which is both unhealthy and unproductive.

Taking Time to Recover

Once you've taken action, allow yourself to *step*

away completely for a significant period—6 to 12 months if possible.

Use this time to:

- **Rest and recharge**: Travel, enjoy the sun, and indulge in things that make you genuinely happy.
- **Reflect**: Think deeply about what you want to do next. What excites you? What aligns with your current values and goals?
- **Rebuild**: Mentally and physically prepare for the next chapter of your life.

For me, after ending a 13-year career that consumed my heart and soul, I took a year off. It was one of the best decisions I've ever made. That time away helped me recover and prepared me for my next adventure in property—a completely different but equally fulfilling journey.

Burnout is Serious

Burnout isn't just a phase; it can be dangerous.

Left unchecked, it can lead to severe health issues and damage relationships. Learn to recognise when you're approaching your limits and don't let pride or fear keep you stuck in a situation past its expiration date.

Your health, happiness, and well-being are irreplaceable. Take care of yourself first, and you'll be better prepared for whatever comes next.

Strategies for Dealing with Burnout

1. Prioritise Rest & Recovery

Burnout doesn't resolve itself—you need **intentional downtime.** Schedule time to completely disconnect from work, whether it's a short break, a vacation, or a sabbatical. Give your mind and body the **rest they need.**

2. Set Boundaries & Protect Your Energy

Define **clear working hours** and stick to them. Learn to say no to **non-essential commitments** and delegate tasks where possible. Protecting your time ensures you don't deplete your mental and physical reserves

3. Focus on What You Control

Stress often comes from trying to control things outside your influence. Identify what's **truly within your power** and let go of the rest. Redirect your energy to actions that create positive change.

4. Implement a Wellness Routine

Prioritise **exercise, sleep, and nutrition.** Incorporate meditation, journalling, or mindfulness practices to reduce stress and regain clarity. **A healthy body supports a resilient mind.**

5. Seek Professional Support

Burnout is serious. If you're struggling to cope, don't hesitate to seek guidance from **a mentor, coach, or mental health professional.** Sometimes an outside perspective can help you navigate difficult decisions more effectively.

6. Reassess Your Goals & Business Model

Ask yourself: **Is my current lifestyle sustainable?** If your workload is unsustainable, it might be time to **pivot, delegate, or restructure your business** to reduce pressure. Long-term success depends on **a balanced approach.**

7. Find Joy Beyond Work

Make time for **hobbies, family, and passions** outside of business. Engaging in **creative or social activities** helps restore energy and perspective, making you more effective when you return to work.

Taking control of burnout isn't just about surviving—it's about thriving. Prioritise your well-being, set boundaries, and build a life where success doesn't come at the cost of your health.

Strategy 47

AI: You Can't Ignore It

"The best way to predict the future is to create it." - Peter Drucker

Let me start with a confession: I'm a novice when it comes to using AI—aren't we all to some extent? But even as a beginner, I've found it fascinating and incredibly useful. The truth is, I'm probably only scratching the surface of its potential, using maybe less than 00000.1% of what's possible.

The Speed and Power of AI

The tasks that once took me a day now take 15 minutes—yes, 15 minutes! It's hard to believe how much time AI can save. Whether it's writing, data analysis, scheduling, or brainstorming, AI has made me faster, more efficient, and more productive.

While there's a lot of discussion about the potential dangers of AI—and I agree that in the wrong hands it could be harmful—it's impossible to ignore its positive impact. I recently watched a BBC program about how AI solved a complex protein puzzle that had baffled scientists for years. This breakthrough could lead to life-saving medical advances.

In the right hands, AI has the potential to revolutionise humanity:

- How we solve problems.
- How we save lives.
- How we work and live more efficiently.

Why Your Business Needs AI

For your business, I strongly recommend embracing AI. Here's how you can start:

1. **Bring in an AI Specialist**

Hire or consult with someone who understands AI deeply. Let them analyse your processes, systems, and workflows. Often, there are inefficiencies we don't even notice because we've accepted them as "just the way things are."

2. **Redesign Your Workflows**

With an expert's help, you can reshape outdated or manual systems. This can do the following:

- Reduce costs.
- Save time.
- Increase accuracy.

- Automate repetitive tasks.

3. **Free Up Your Team for Meaningful Work**
AI doesn't replace people; it complements them. By handling mundane tasks, AI allows your team to focus on creative, engaging, and revenue-generating activities.

Embrace the Future

AI is no longer "coming"—it's here, and it's changing everything. From personal productivity to life-altering discoveries, its potential is enormous. The businesses that embrace it will have a significant advantage over those that resist it.

Take action now. Invest the time to understand how AI can help you, your team, and your customers. The future is already unfolding, and it's powered by AI.

Action point: Get a referral to an AI specialist who will take a look at your business and its processes. Ask them to come up with a new plan which embraces AI. Free up your team's time so that they can focus on more advantageous work.

If you can go to an AI conference to learn what happening right now and what's possible. I promise you will be amazed.

Don't say to yourself "AI can't help my business," be open-minded.

Strategy 48

Urgency Fuels Action, Vision Shapes Destiny

"Speed is useful only if you are running in the right direction." - Joel Barker

Early in my career, my natural tendency was to move fast. I'd set ambitious goals, create targets, and chase them with relentless urgency and energy. I wanted everything yesterday – both in my business and personal life. While this drive helped me achieve a lot, it also led to mistakes and hasty decisions that could have been avoided.

Over time, I've trained myself to take a more strategic approach: play the long game.

Why the Long Game Matters

Playing the long game is like playing chess:

- You need a clear strategy.
- You should always know your next 5 moves.
- But you don't act until the timing is right.

A long-term plan gives you focus, discipline, and perspective. It prevents impulsive decisions and ensures every action aligns with your broader vision.

What is the long game? It could be a 7-year business plan or a significant personal milestone. Whatever it is, it's about building something meaningful and sustainable rather than chasing short-term wins.

Balancing Urgency with Patience

While the long game is critical, urgency is equally important, especially when leading a team. Urgency creates momentum and drives action.

Here's how you can balance the two:

1. **Set the Vision**

Make sure your team understands the long-term goal. Clearly articulate where you're heading and, importantly, what's in it for them.

2. Break It Down

Break the long-term plan into short-term targets. These smaller, achievable milestones create focus and give your team a sense of accomplishment.

3. **Celebrate Progress**
Acknowledge and reward your team when they hit short-term goals. It keeps the energy high and reinforces the importance of incremental success.

4. **Stay Patient and Strategic**
While you create urgency for day-to-day tasks, don't lose sight of the bigger picture. Be prepared to pivot when necessary but always evaluate how each decision fits into the long-term strategy.

The Takeaway

The balance between urgency and patience is a powerful tool in business and life. Urgency keeps you moving; patience ensures you're moving in the right direction.

Train yourself and your team to think strategically but act decisively. The long game is not about slow progress—it's about making smart moves at the right time to achieve extraordinary results.

Strategy 49

Failure Can Be a Gift

"Success is not final, failure is not fatal: it is the courage to continue that counts." - Winston Churchill

FROM A BROKEN LADDER TO A NEW PATH

Where do I even start with this thought? In the U.S., there's a cultural sentiment that if you haven't failed big at least once, you haven't truly been in business and lived. Some even say that someone who hasn't experienced significant failure isn't yet truly seasoned. While I don't fully subscribe to those ideas, I do understand where they come from.

From personal experience, I can confidently say my biggest growth moments came from my most challenging times. It's when the pressure is on, and it feels like bullets are flying at you from every direction, that you discover who you really are.

When the Property Company Collapsed

I've been there. Our property company went under, and almost everyone ran for the hills. My business partner disappeared to a remote village in France, never to be heard from again. I was left standing in the rubble, facing the fallout with John and Alan T.

While that failure was brutal, it also became a defining moment for me. Success is enjoyable, of course, but it doesn't push you in the same way adversity does.

Real growth happens when the stakes are high, and everything is on the line.

Why Failure is a Gift

1. **It Reveals Who You Are**
Success can sometimes mask your weaknesses, but failure lays them bare. It shows you where you need to grow and forces you to confront your limitations.

2. **It Teaches You What *Not* to Do**
Knowing what to avoid is often more valuable than knowing what to pursue. In my darkest moments, I've relied on trusted advisors to point me away from potential disasters. Their wisdom was like a compass—priceless, as long as I listened.

3. **It Builds Resilience**
Failure tests your confidence and resolve. It can be devastating, but it also gives you a sharper focus. The lessons from failure don't fade; they're seared into your memory, driving you to make better decisions in the future.

4. **It Prevents Complacency**
Pain is a powerful motivator. Failure can wake you up in ways that success never will. It pushes you to evolve, adapt, and never make the same mistake twice.

The Takeaway

Failure can feel like the end of the world, but it's often just the beginning of something transformative. The pain may be immediate and raw, but the lessons are enduring and invaluable.

Learn to view failure not as the opposite of success but as a crucial step toward it.

When you fail, ask yourself:

- What went wrong?
- What can I learn?
- How can I grow?

Remember, failure doesn't define you—how you respond to it does. Embrace the gift of failure and use it to fuel your next success.

Get Ready, There Will be a Storm

Strategy 50

If You're Going to Go Big, Get Fit

"The higher your energy level, the more efficient your body. The more efficient your body, the better you feel and the more you will use your talent to produce outstanding results." - Tony Robbins

I can't stress enough what it takes to build a big business. I've mentioned blood, sweat, and tears, but I left out two crucial elements: **fitness and energy.** Without them, you won't last in the marathon of entrepreneurship, especially when it demands 5 AM starts and late nights for 3–10 years straight.

To go all out for such an intense period, you need to be **healthy, fit, and energised.** You might still reach your destination without prioritising fitness, but at what cost? Burnout, fatigue, and even health issues could come knocking.

Why Fitness is Non-Negotiable

1. **It Fuels Your Energy**
Long hours, high stakes, and relentless problem-solving require peak energy levels. Exercise and good nutrition will give you the stamina you need to push through tough days and weeks.

2. **It Sharpens Your Mind**

A healthy body leads to a sharper, more focused mind. Cardio, strength training, or even yoga—whatever you choose—will help flood your brain with ideas and improve your decision-making ability.

3. **It Builds Resilience**

Fitness teaches discipline and perseverance, two traits you need to weather the ups and downs of building a business. It's not just physical—it's mental conditioning too.

Find What Works for You

I'm not here to tell you to join a gym, although I personally do. What matters is finding a fitness routine that works for you and **sticking to it.**

- **Cardio** to keep your heart and endurance strong.
- **Strength training** to build resilience and confidence.
- **Healthy eating** to avoid the energy-draining effects of poor nutrition.

It doesn't have to be complicated—walking, cycling, swimming, or even playing a sport can be just as effective as hitting the weights.

The Takeaway

It's impossible to perform at your peak when your body is flooded with junk food, stress, and exhaustion. Prioritise your health starting **today**—not when it's convenient or when you've "made it."

Building an amazing business starts with you being at your best, physically and mentally.

So, here's your challenge:

- Find a fitness program.
- Commit to it.
- Give yourself 100% to the process.

Your business—and your life—depends on it. Go for it!

Strategy 51

The Power of Knowledge

"If you want to be successful, find someone who has achieved the results you want and copy what they do, and you'll achieve the same results." - Tony Robbins

Since my early 20s, I've been an avid reader of self-development books and autobiographies. There's something incredibly motivating about reading someone's life story—whether it's uplifting or filled with challenges. Each one offers valuable lessons and insights. Today, I am listening to a book by the amazing **David Goggins, "Can't Hurt Me" WOW that's all I can say! Talk about being single minded, determined and a winner.**

The Power of Self-Development Books

In 2018, **Robin Sharma** published ***The 5 AM Club***. I bought it immediately, read a few pages, and put it down, thinking, I don't get it...*This isn't for me.* Fast forward to 2023, and for some reason, I was drawn to it again. This time, it clicked and everything made perfect sense.

Here's the point: **Sometimes you're not ready for a book, and that's okay.** Other times, you read it, take away one message, and then re-read it years later and find a completely different lesson. That's the magic of self-development books—they grow with you as you grow.

Joining the *5 AM Club* has genuinely changed my life. I'm more productive, focused, and energised than ever before. It's an incredible book, but only if you're ready to absorb its wisdom.

Books and Podcasts: Fuel for the Mind

I recommend books and podcasts to all my clients.

- **Books** inspire new ideas and perspectives.
- **Podcasts** connect you to thought leaders and real-world advice that can change your mindset in minutes.

Personally, I prefer **Audible**—listening to books while walking or commuting works better for me than holding a physical copy.

The Power of Reading & Lifelong Learning

"Once you stop learning, you start dying." - **Albert Einstein**

Reading and acquiring new knowledge isn't just about personal growth—it's a competitive advantage. The world is evolving at an unprecedented pace, and those who continuously learn are the ones who stay ahead. The best leaders, entrepreneurs, and visionaries are voracious readers and lifelong learners.

Why Reading & Learning Matter

- **Expands Your Perspective:** Exposure to new ideas broadens your thinking, allowing you to innovate and solve problems more effectively.
- **Accelerates Personal & Professional Growth:** The more you learn, the more valuable you become in your industry and life.
- **Helps You Adapt & Stay Relevant:** In a

fast-changing world, knowledge is power. Staying informed gives you an edge.

- **Improves Decision-Making:** A well-informed mind makes better, more strategic decisions based on insights and experience.

Action Points: Building a Habit of Continuous Learning

Step 1: Commit to Daily Reading

Set aside at least **15–30 minutes daily** to read. Whether it's books, articles, or industry reports, consistent learning compounds over time. I do most of mine in the bath!

Step 2: Diversify Your Learning Sources

Read books across multiple disciplines—**business, psychology, history, and leadership**. Listen to podcasts, take online courses, and attend industry events for a well-rounded knowledge base.

Step 3: Apply What You Learn

Knowledge without action is wasted. After reading a book or learning something new, **implement at least one key takeaway** into your business or life.

Step 4: Teach Others

One of the best ways to retain knowledge is to **teach it to someone else**. Share insights with your team, write about what you've learned, or mentor others.

Step 5: Surround Yourself with Lifelong Learners

Engage with people who challenge and inspire you to grow. Join book clubs, mastermind groups, or networking communities where continuous learning is the norm.

Make reading and learning a priority, and you'll unlock new levels of success, creativity, and wisdom. The more you know, the more opportunities you create!

Strategy 52

Don't let your Mouth Write a Cheque your Brain Can't Cash – Ben

"Stay hungry, stay foolish." - Steve Jobs

Years ago, I made a fool of myself in front of my peers, largely because my ego got the better of me.

There was a guy in the business named Ben. He was doing well, and there was a healthy dose of competition between us—or at least it should have been healthy. In hindsight, I let it get to me more than I should have.

One day, during a team meeting with about 20 of us in a large boardroom, we were discussing sales targets for the next quarter. Ben, as usual, arrived late, which annoyed me. He had a habit of being late, but as the golden boy of the moment, his tardiness was often overlooked.

Ben burst into the room with his trademark big smile and confidently proclaimed, "The future of communication is EMAIL!"

At the time, email wasn't widely known or used in mainstream business. I remember thinking, *What an idiot.*

And what did I do? I shot him down in flames. I tried to make him look foolish in front of everyone. The problem was, I was the one who ended up looking foolish.

My need to compete clouded my judgement. Email, as we all know it now, has become the cornerstone of modern communication. Ben had done his homework, and he was looking toward the future, while I was stuck in the present.

Over time, I came to like Ben a lot. He was a bit goofy, but he was a genuinely nice guy who worked hard to achieve his goals.

The lesson here? Always think before you speak, especially in front of others. Healthy competition can be great, but it should never cross the line into pettiness. And most importantly, keep one eye on tomorrow, not just today.

Get Ready, There Will be a Storm

Strategy 53

Your Subconscious Mind and Your Mastermind Group

"You are the average of the five people you spend the most time with." - Jim Rohn

The concept of a **mastermind group** was popularised by Napoleon Hill in his 1937 classic, *Think and Grow Rich*. Hill described it as a "friendly alliance" of individuals who come together to share knowledge, experiences, and ideas, helping one another achieve greater success.

The Power of Collective Thinking

Hill believed that when like-minded individuals collaborate, they create a unique synergy – a combined energy and intelligence capable of accomplishing far more than any individual could alone.

A mastermind group provides:

- **New perspectives**
- **Encouragement and accountability**
- **Practical guidance for growth**

This concept is timeless and has transformed how leaders and entrepreneurs approach challenges.

Create Your Own Virtual Mastermind Group

Years ago, I was introduced to a twist on this idea that has profoundly impacted my business and personal life.

Here's how you can create your **virtual mastermind group**:

1. **Identify Areas for Improvement**

Think of 8–10 traits, skills, or areas in your life you'd like to improve. Examples might include:

- Boosting your confidence
- Becoming more dynamic or outgoing
- Increasing energy and fitness
- Improving financial acumen
- Becoming more charitable or giving
- Achieving balance and calmness
- Inspiring others
- Taking calculated risks

2. **Select Your "Mentors"**

Choose someone who excels in each of these areas.

They don't have to be real; your subconscious mind doesn't distinguish between real and imagined.

For example, when I need to be bold, brave, and dynamic, I might think of **James Bond.** For balance and peace, I might imagine **the Dalai Lama, as for being creative and business Richard Branson. For leadership, motivation, and peak performance Tony Robbins. Never giving up, David Goggins, Adventure and not being scared of anything Bear Grylls!**

Who you choose is up to you; it's your mastermind group, not mine! Who inspires you?

3. **Draw Your Mastermind Group**
Draw a circle with **your name in the centre.** Surround it with smaller circles, each labelled with a trait and the person who inspires you in that area.

4. **Consult Your Virtual Group Daily**
When faced with a challenge, ask yourself:

What would [mentor's name] do in this situation?

Step into their mindset and act as they would.

Why This Works

Your subconscious mind is incredibly powerful. By regularly visualising and consulting this "team," you train yourself to adopt the traits and habits you admire in others. It's a mental exercise that aligns your actions with your goals.

The 3-Month Challenge

For the next 90 days, use your virtual mastermind group daily. Reflect on how it influences your decisions and mindset. You'll find yourself acting with more confidence, clarity, and purpose.

Crazy as it sounds, it works—and it works really well. Make it a habit and see the difference it makes in your life and business!

Strategy 54

Tim and Christmas Eve – Never Give Up When You're Raising Money

"Persistence overshadows even talent as the most valuable resource shaping the quality of life." - Tony Robbins

Let me set the scene. I was working with a team of entrepreneurs in London, helping them create a strategy to attract their **ideal clients – law partners earning over £250k a year.**

After extensive research, I proposed an events program designed to resonate with this exclusive audience.

Here are the three carefully chosen events:
1. **Fly fishing**
2. **Golf**
3. **Clay shooting**

The founders loved the idea. Within 4 weeks, I had planned every detail: dates, venues, and costs.

The total budget for the program came to **£250,000.**

The Setback

We had identified potential sponsors and felt confident we'd secure the funding.

Then, disaster struck. The companies we planned to approach could no longer legally allocate sponsorship money to third-party programs like ours due to new regulations.

It felt like a dead end. The obvious choice was to abandon the project and chalk it up as a loss. But giving up isn't in my nature.

Persistence in Action

I started knocking on every possible door, calling contacts, pitching the idea, and asking for support. The biggest hurdle? **It was December.** Most companies had already allocated their marketing budgets for the following year. I received rejection after rejection.

Still, I refused to give up.

A Christmas Miracle

Then, a glimmer of hope appeared: Tim, was a serial entrepreneur and a friend of the company. I was given the green light to reach out, and to my surprise, his PA managed to fit me into his schedule on **Christmas Eve** – in his Mayfair office at 2pm, no less.

I couldn't believe he was working on Christmas Eve, let alone willing to meet me. On the way to his office, I set my expectations low. I hoped to secure **£50k or maybe £100k**, enough to start the program and buy time to raise the rest in January.

What happened next was extraordinary. Tim loved the idea. He immediately committed to funding the **entire £250k.**

Lessons Learnt

This experience was a powerful reminder of the importance of **resilience and persistence** when raising money. There were so many moments when giving up felt like the logical choice. But I kept going, and it paid off.

- **Timing doesn't have to be perfect.** Even

on Christmas Eve, there's an opportunity to find the right supporter.

- **Don't be afraid to ask.** You might be surprised who says yes.
- **Persistence wins.** Keep knocking on doors, no matter how many close in your face.

If you're raising money for your business, never give up. You never know which conversation will lead to your breakthrough. Sometimes, miracles happen when you least expect them.

Be a honey badger, determined, persistent and never give up.

Get Ready, There Will be a Storm

Strategy 55

Know Your Numbers or Die

"If you don't know your numbers, you don't know your business." - Marcus Lemonis

One of the most critical aspects of raising money is understanding your finances. Yet, very rarely do I meet business owners who truly have a handle on their numbers when presenting to investors.

This is not a criticism. Why? Because **investors often look at your business and financials differently than you do.**

Where Most Business Owners Stand

Most business owners can:

- Tell you where they are today financially.
- Tell you where they have been historically
- Run decent management accounts.
- Have a general understanding of their cash flow.
- Possibly know their true cost of sales.
- Maybe even know their customer acquisition costs.

The real challenge arises when it's time to create **projections for the next 3–5 years.**

Investors Will Test Your Assumptions

When creating assumptions and projections, many business owners rely on their accountants to produce the numbers. These accountants often base their work on assumptions provided by the business owner. Unfortunately, in my experience, many accountants rarely challenge or test those assumptions. Why? most business owners do not set them the task properly. Also, creating a set of projections for say 3–5 years takes time. Your accountant needs to be paid.

If you do not have the funds to pay your accountant, today ask them to take the money required in instalments or better still promise them that you will pay them out of the funds you raise (there is of course risk on their part to this).

Most accountants will input the data/assumptions you give them and produce a polished set of financials for you (**many accountants are excellent by the way**).

The issue? **Investors will test you—and some will test you hard.** If you don't know your numbers or can't defend your assumptions, it can derail your pitch.

Steps to Take

1. **Test Your Assumptions**

Before handing anything to your accountant or business advisor, ensure your assumptions have been stress-tested.

Drill deep into your data and projections. If you project a 20% increase in revenue next year, ask yourself how realistic that is. Where is it coming from? What resources will you need to make it happen?

2. **Integrate All Elements**

Your financial projections should be fully

integrated. Revenue growth, cost of sales, marketing expenses, and operational costs should all align. Everything needs to make sense as a cohesive whole.

3. **Own Your Numbers**
Know your financials like the back of your hand. If an investor challenges your assumptions, you need to confidently explain why you believe they are accurate.

4. **Prepare for Questions**
Practice answering tough questions with your team or advisors. What will you say if an investor questions your profit margins, growth rates, or cost structure?

The Common Pitfall

Too many times, I've been in meetings where a founder was asked a question about their projections and couldn't answer it. Instead, they deflected by saying something like, *"I'm not sure; my accountant put those together."*

This response never sits well with investors. Why? Because it shows a lack of preparation and ownership. Investors want to back founders who **know their business inside out.**

The Bottom Line

Own your numbers.

Your financials are the foundation of your pitch. If you don't fully understand them, it signals to investors that you might not fully understand your business.

When you know your numbers, you'll not only impress investors but also have the confidence to steer your business in the right direction.

Strategy 56

Keep Your Business Partner Real Close

"Trust is good, but control is better." - Andy Grove, former CEO of Intel

Over the years, I've been involved in many ventures and businesses where I had partners. When partnerships work well, they can be extraordinary, bringing out the best in everyone involved. I firmly believe in the power of collaboration and that you can achieve more by working in a team.

However, when partnerships go wrong – when objectives differ or trust breaks down – it can be disastrous. I should know I've been through hell with one in particular.

Trust, but Verify

Here's what I've learnt:

- **Trust your gut.** If you feel your partner is not being honest or their goals aren't aligned with yours, address it immediately. A small issue can grow into a big problem if left unchecked. *Kill monsters while they're small.*
- Never trust anyone with **everything.** This doesn't mean being paranoid; it means

being smart and protecting yourself and your business.

Practical Steps to Safeguard Yourself

1. **Maintain Significant Control of Your Company/Partnership**
   - Ensure you are a director and shareholder in the company.
   - Confirm you are officially listed as a "Person with Significant Control" (PSC) in company filings.

2. **Secure Bank Accounts**
   - Have direct access to the company's bank accounts.
   - Keep your passwords secure and ensure limits are set on how much any one person can spend without approval.
   - Draft an **Expenses Policy Document** stating the maximum spend without co-signature, and have all partners sign it.

3. **Admin Rights**
    - Have administrator rights to all company email accounts and systems.
    - Without admin rights, an unscrupulous partner could block your access, leaving you powerless.

4. **Loan Agreements**
    - Ensure no loans can be taken out in the company's name without your signature on the agreement. Put this in writing and have all partners sign it.

5. **Partnership/Shareholder Agreements**
    - Create a clear and detailed **Partnership Agreement** or **Shareholders' Agreement.**
    - Outline responsibilities, decision-making processes, and dispute-resolution methods.

Why This Matters

Even the best partnerships can encounter challenges. By putting safeguards in place, you reduce the risk of mismanagement, dishonesty, or misaligned objectives. Being proactive ensures that everyone remains accountable and aligned with the company's goals.

Final Thought

Good partnerships are worth their weight in gold, but they require trust and transparency. While it's important to trust your partners, you must also protect yourself. **Be in control. Don't trust anyone with everything.** It's not about mistrust—it's about ensuring the success and security of your venture.

Strategy 57

Networking and Empowering Your Team

"Success in business is all about people... You can spend an enormous amount of time building a product, but in the end, it all comes down to people." - Mark Zuckerberg

Networking is such an essential skill that can be developed and refined.

While you might think it comes naturally to salespeople, my experience tells me otherwise. Even seasoned sales professionals sometimes struggle to effectively navigate a room and identify key connections.

It's not enough for just your sales team to be great at networking, everyone in your organisation should be equipped with this skill, even your admin team.

Every person in your business represents your brand and has the potential to open new doors.

Learning from the Best

A few years ago, I had the privilege of being introduced to **Tracey Currel** (formerly Smolinski), often referred to as the "**Queen of Networking and Connections**".

Tracey has an exceptional ability to teach

people how to network effectively. She is a bestselling author and runs **Introbiz,** an innovative B2B networking organisation.

I recently asked Tracey for her insights on how to empower teams through networking, and here's what she shared:

Tracey's Tips for Networking Excellence

1. Preparation is Key
Research attendees and companies beforehand. Have a clear goal for who you'd like to meet and why by creating and planning a strategy before you even attend an event.

2. Make It About Them
Networking is not about selling; it's about building win-win relationships. Ask open-ended questions to learn about the other person's business, challenges, and goals, so that you can help them further. If you don't ask questions, how do you know how you can serve them?

3. Confidence is Contagious

Teach your team to walk into a room with confidence, make eye contact, and smile.

First impressions matter. People are more likely to be drawn to positive uplifting people than negative Nora's.

4. The Power of Follow-Up

Networking doesn't end when the event is over. Ensure your team understands the importance of following up within 24 hours. Send a personalised message to strengthen the connection and remind them where you met them. The fortune is in the follow-up.

5. Empower Everyone to Represent the Brand

Whether it's the CEO or the receptionist, every team member should have a clear understanding of your company's mission, values, key messages and how you solve problems.

6. Listen for Opportunities to Help

Listening is such a skill and so many people are

so keen to talk about themselves that they forget and just plough ahead.

By listening to what others are saying, you can identify and spot ways to help them, and if you can't help them, you can introduce them to someone else who can help.

7. Training Your Team

Consider investing in networking workshops or bringing in a professional. Tailored training can boost confidence, improve communication skills, and ultimately lead to better business relationships.

Final Thought

Networking is a powerful tool that can drive growth and open doors to limitless opportunities you didn't even know existed.

The law of attraction is so important when networking. You want people to gravitate to you.

Tracey says:
"What do people say about you when you are not there? Will they promote and recommend you when your zone of genius is discussed?

The aim is that when you are not present, they will promote and recommend you in a positive light and hopefully bring you more referrals and recommendations."

When you empower your entire team to network on your behalf, you create a ripple effect of connections and goodwill that can benefit your business for years to come.

Make sure you reward your people for walking new clients through the door.

"Networking is not about collecting contacts; it's about building long-lasting win-win relationships." Teach your team this principle, and watch your business thrive.

Networking and building relationships are never about you, it's about what YOU can DO for other people.

We all need attention and time, so give people your time and attention, and show that you are listening and that you care, you will win them over so much more and grow your connections that will last for life.

I would love to hear about your networking successes. If you have a question or a challenge that I can help you with, email me at info@introbiz.co.uk and I will do my best to help and support you.

Excited to share your stories with me.

Strategy 58

Seek Out the Best Financial Advisers

"Surround yourself with people who are smarter than you, give them the freedom to make decisions, and watch your success multiply." - Richard Branson

Having the right financial advice is essential, and I speak from experience as someone who was regulated for 13 years in this field. One of the key lessons I've learnt is that no single financial adviser is an expert in all areas you'll likely need assistance with.

To get the best results, look for a **firm with a team of advisers who specialise in various areas**—such as pensions, investments, tax planning, and insurance. This way, you can receive well-rounded advice tailored to your specific goals, all under one roof.

What to Look for in a Financial Adviser

1. **Independence**
Choose advisers who are independent and not tied to any particular products or providers. This ensures their advice is unbiased and in your best interest.

2. **Qualifications**
Check that your advisers have top-tier

qualifications, such as the Chartered Financial Planner designation or equivalent.

3. **Fee-Based Services**

Work with advisers who charge fees for their services rather than earning commissions on product sales. This structure ensures their focus is on your goals, not their earnings.

The Importance of a Written Financial Plan

A great financial adviser will always **start with the end in mind** and work backwards to create a roadmap for your financial future. This plan should be clear, realistic, and tailored to your personal goals. Importantly, it must be in writing so you can track your progress and stay focused.

One of the biggest mistakes people make is **underestimating how much they'll need to retire comfortably or to slow down later in life**. A good adviser will help you plan for these realities and ensure you're on track to meet your long-term needs. Your plan needs to be inflation-proofed.

Don't Overlook Property Investments

While most financial advisers won't typically guide you on property investment, I firmly believe that owning investment properties should be part of your **wealth accumulation strategy**. Properties can provide steady cash flow, capital growth, and diversification. Plus, unlike a fund, you own the property and have total control.

If this aligns with your goals, consider consulting a **property investment specialist** alongside your financial adviser to create a balanced approach to building wealth.

Final Thought

Financial planning doesn't have to be overwhelming. The key is to work with the right team of advisers who bring expertise, independence, and integrity to the table. Start now, get your plan in place, and ensure your financial future is secure.

Strategy 59

Real Bullets

"Fuck me real bullets." -
Bob Patmore

In life, there are things people tell you that just stick. Bob Patmore is an entrepreneur. He has a unique way of explaining concepts that leave a lasting impression. He is a master at painting vivid mental pictures, an incredible man manager, motivator, and public speaker.

One of Bob's analogies still makes me smile to this day.

Bob explained that when people work together for the first time, much of what they talk about is focused on the future—which is natural. However, some individuals let their egos get the better of them. They bluff, they brag, they make bold claims about what they'll accomplish.

Bob likened this behaviour to firing rubber bullets. They're loud and flashy but ultimately harmless—rubber bullets won't kill you.

Then, as Bob would say, "Once the business takes off and those same people have their feet held to the fire, they often crumble under real pressure." And in his unforgettable tone, I can still hear him exclaiming, *"FUCK me real bullets!"*

I'm laughing even as I write this because Bob had such a way with words.

So, the next time you encounter a bluffer or a bragger, just think, *"FUCK me real bullets!"* It'll remind you to separate talk from action—and trust only those who deliver under pressure.

Get Ready, There Will be a Storm

Strategy 60

Golden Nuggets and Hidden Gems-Acquiring Businesses

"The big money is not in the buying and selling, but in the waiting." - Charlie Munger

Acquiring complementary businesses that are undervalued and poorly run can be a highly lucrative strategy when executed thoughtfully.

Here's a step-by-step guide to maximise your chances of success:

1. Identify Strategic Alignment

Look for businesses that align with or enhance your core operations. These could be suppliers, distributors, competitors, or companies offering complementary products or services. The goal is to create synergies that improve your overall business value.

Example: If you own a logistics company, acquiring a packaging business could add value by offering end-to-end solutions for clients.

2. Evaluate the Market Opportunity

Study the industry dynamics, customer demand, and potential growth areas. Ensure the business has a viable market even if it's underperforming. Pay attention to shifts in technology, regulation, or consumer trends that might give the business an edge post-turnaround.

3. Look for Red Flags and Hidden Gems
Key indicators of poorly managed businesses include:

- High staff turnover.
- Lack of process efficiency or outdated technology.
- Owner disengagement or lack of motivation.
- Poor financial management, marketing, or customer service.
- Look for negative comments on social media from ex-staff members.

These issues, while challenging, often provide opportunities for improvement. Look beyond the symptoms to evaluate the root causes and determine if they're fixable under new ownership.

4. Build a Deal Pipeline

Network with business brokers, accountants, and lawyers who specialise in business sales. Attend industry events, connect with struggling owners, and leverage word-of-mouth referrals to uncover opportunities.

5. Understand the Business's Value

Conduct a thorough valuation to identify whether the business is truly undervalued. Use methods like:

- **Asset valuation:** Identify tangible and intangible assets.
- **Revenue multiples:** Compare with industry standards.
- **Discounted cash flow (DCF):** Assess future earning potential.

Look for "hidden value," such as underutilised assets, valuable customer contracts, or intellectual property.

6. Perform Deep Due Diligence

Examine the business thoroughly before making an offer.

- **Financial health:** Review balance sheets, cash flow, debt, and profitability.
- **Legal and tax compliance:** Check for charges/liens, lawsuits, or tax issues.
- **Operational efficiency:** Evaluate key processes, systems, and staff.
- **Customer and supplier relationships:** Ensure these relationships are salvageable or transferable.

7. Craft a Vision for Turnaround

Before acquiring, identify how you'll transform the business. Ask the following questions:

- What inefficiencies can you fix?
- Can you reduce costs or renegotiate supplier agreements?
- How will you improve revenue (e.g., cross-selling with your existing business, rebranding, marketing)?

Will you keep plant and equipment?

Will you need a new premises? Can you

convert the existing premises (if there is one)? There are many more considerations.

A clear plan will not only guide the turnaround but also help you secure financing if needed.

8. Negotiate Favourable Terms

Use the business's poor performance as leverage in negotiations. Look for opportunities to:

- **Structure earn-outs:** Pay part of the price based on future performance.
- **Seek seller financing:** The current owner might finance a portion of the deal.
- **Negotiate warranties and indemnities:** Protect yourself from unforeseen liabilities.

9. Retain Key Talent and Knowledge

Engage with the existing team to ensure continuity and smooth transition. Identify the most valuable employees and keep them on board during the transformation. Often, long-term staff have critical knowledge about the business.

10. Integrate and Optimise

Post-acquisition, focus on rapid integration.

- Consolidate operations with your existing business where possible.
- Streamline costs and processes to boost efficiency.
- Implement strong leadership and clear goals.
- Focus on rebuilding customer trust and improving service quality.

11. Consider the Emotional Angle

Owners of poorly run businesses often feel emotionally drained. Approach them with empathy during negotiations. Position yourself as someone who will preserve their legacy and improve what they've built.

12. Secure Financing Options

If you need funding, explore:

- Bank loans or lines of credit.
- Angel investors or venture capitalists.
- Government loans and grants.

13. Leverage Tax Benefits

Work with a tax professional to understand if there are tax advantages to acquiring a struggling business, such as using net operating losses (NOLs) to offset future taxable income (or the equivalent in the US).

14. Prepare for Risk Management

Mitigate risks by:

- Using non-compete agreements with the seller.
- Insuring key assets or contracts.
- Building contingency plans for potential obstacles.

15. Focus on ROI, Not Just Cost

While finding a low-cost acquisition is appealing, always evaluate the potential return on investment (ROI). An undervalued business that aligns with your long-term strategy is more valuable than one that's simply cheap.

Final Thoughts

Acquiring and turning around an undervalued business requires diligence, strategic vision, and operational expertise. Be patient and focused—often the biggest gains come from creating value where others saw none. Stay committed to your plan, and the results will follow. Remember what Charlie advises: **The big money is not in the buying and selling, but in the waiting.**

Conclusion

The Storm is Coming - Will You Be Ready?

You've now explored 60 business strategies and ideas—many forged through real-world challenges, battle-tested in the heat of experience. These strategies are designed to help you not just survive but thrive in any financial climate. Not all strategies will apply to you and your business but all of the core ones do, focus on these.

Come back to this book as your business grows, there are words of wisdom here that will resonate on a different day.

What you do next is entirely up to you.

The world is unpredictable. Storms – financial, economic, and personal – will come. You can't control when they arrive, but you can control how prepared you are.

A Quick Recap

- **Never Overleverage:** Protect your financial foundation so you don't get wiped out when the next crisis hits.
- **Build Your Billboard:** Make sure your business stands out, whether you're raising money, attracting clients, or growing your brand.
- **Surround Yourself with Giants:** Your network is your net worth. Find mentors, team members, and partners who elevate your business.
- **Take Calculated Risks:** Ships are safest

in the harbour, but that's not what they were built for. When opportunity knocks, be ready to take action.

- **Kill Problems Early:** Small issues become monsters if left unchecked. Deal with toxic people, bad hires, and financial leaks before they grow.
- **Stay Relentless:** Most people quit when success is inches away. Keep pumping the pump—the water is closer than you think.

Your Next Steps

This book isn't just meant to be read. It's meant to be used.

Take Action: Pick five strategies from this book that resonate with you most and implement them this month.

Review Your Business & Finances: Where are your weak spots? Where are you over exposed? What small shifts can make you more resilient?

Surround Yourself with Great People: Who are the mentors, investors, and advisors you need in your corner?

Give Back. Success isn't just about making money—it's about making a difference. If you got value from this book, consider donating to Smile Train and helping change a child's life.

A Personal Thank You

I wrote this book to share everything I've learnt—not just about business, but about overcoming challenges, adapting, and coming back stronger.

If even one idea from this book helps you think bigger, act bolder, or protect your business, then my mission is accomplished.

I would love to hear your thoughts, feedback, and success stories. Drop me an email on tom@tom-capital.co.uk or visit tom-capital.co.uk to stay connected.

Live with passion, and I hope to see you someday at one of my courses or events.

Stay strong, stay ready, and when the storm comes – be the one who thrives.

Tom Luttrell.

Smile Train

Good morning, Tom.

Thank you for providing further details about your soon-to-be-published book. The best link to put in the book would be our main website address, smiletrain.org.uk. I have also drafted a short paragraph which can be put in the book to share more information about **Smile Train** and how donations would support our work.

'Smile Train is the world's largest cleft-focused organisation, with a sustainable and local model of supporting surgery and other forms of essential, comprehensive care. Every three minutes, another baby is born struggling to breathe, speak, and eat due to a cleft.

By supporting Smile Train, you could help to provide access to free cleft treatment to children in need, and ultimately the opportunity for a healthy and productive life.

If you have any questions or further requests, please get in touch and I will be happy to help.

Kind regards,
Jonathan.
Senior Manager

Appendix

In this section, I've compiled my top 15 tips addressing areas where my clients often seek the most guidance. I trust you'll find these insights valuable and practical.

Here are 15 actionable tips to boost your confidence:

Mindset and Self-Belief

1. **Identify and Challenge Negative Thoughts**: Replace self-doubt with empowering affirmations. Focus on what you *can* do.

2. **Set Small, Achievable Goals**: Progress breeds confidence. Break big tasks into smaller milestones and celebrate victories.
3. **Embrace Failure as Growth**: See mistakes as learning opportunities rather than setbacks. Confidence comes from resilience.
4. **Visualise Success**: Picture yourself succeeding in situations that make you nervous. Positive visualisation can calm nerves.
5. **Learn from Role Models**: Study confident people you admire and emulate their behaviours and strategies.

Skill-Building and Preparation

1. **Be Prepared**: Whether it's for a meeting, presentation, or social event, preparation reduces uncertainty and builds confidence.
2. **Develop Your Skills**: Mastery in areas important to you will naturally boost your confidence.
3. **Practice Speaking Up**: Start contributing

to small conversations and gradually progress to larger audiences.

Body Language and Appearance

1. **Adopt Confident Postures**: Stand tall, keep your shoulders back, and make eye contact. Your body sends confidence signals to your brain.
2. **Dress for Success**: Wear clothes that make you feel good about yourself—it reflects in how you carry yourself.
3. **Smile More**: Smiling not only makes you appear confident but also tricks your brain into feeling happier.

Habits and Lifestyle

1. **Focus on Self-Care**: A healthy diet, regular exercise, and adequate sleep improve energy levels and self-perception.
2. **Step Outside Your Comfort Zone**: Take on challenges that stretch you, no matter how small—they build self-trust.
3. **Celebrate Your Strengths**: Write a list of your accomplishments and talents.

Reflect on it whenever you feel doubt creeping in.

Social Confidence

1. **Practice Active Listening**: Being fully present in conversations helps you connect better with others, which can boost your confidence in social settings.

Here are 15 essential tips for becoming great at public speaking:

Preparation and Planning

1. **Know Your Audience**: Understand who they are, their needs, and what they expect to gain from your talk. Tailor your message accordingly.
2. **Clarify Your Purpose**: Define the core message or takeaway you want your audience to remember. Build your talk around this.
3. **Practice, Practice, Practice**: Rehearse multiple times – out loud and in front of a mirror or a trusted friend – to refine your delivery.
4. **Prepare an Outline**: Organise your speech with a strong opening, clear main points, and a compelling conclusion.

Delivery Techniques

1. **Start with a Hook**: Grab attention with a story, surprising fact, or question to engage your audience from the start.
2. **Speak Clearly and Slowly**: Enunciate

your words and pace yourself to ensure your message is understood.

3. **Use Pauses Effectively**: Pauses emphasise key points, add drama, and give your audience time to process information.
4. **Engage with Body Language**: Stand tall, use gestures naturally, and make consistent eye contact to exude confidence.

Building Confidence

1. **Practice Positive Visualisation**: Picture yourself speaking confidently and receiving applause. It helps calm pre-speech nerves.
2. **Manage Stage Fright**: Breathe deeply, channel nervous energy into enthusiasm, and remind yourself that nerves are normal.
3. **Know Your Material**: Being thoroughly familiar with your topic reduces anxiety and allows you to speak with authority.

Audience Connection

1. **Interact with Your Audience**: Ask questions, encourage participation, or use humour to keep them engaged and connected.
2. **Adapt to the Room**: Pay attention to audience reactions and adjust your tone, pace, or content if needed.

Enhancing Your Impact

1. **Tell Stories**: People remember stories better than facts. Use relatable anecdotes to illustrate your points.
2. **End with Impact**: Leave a lasting impression with a powerful conclusion, such as a call to action, a memorable quote, or an emotional story.

Here are 15 practical tips to help manage and reduce anxiety:

Immediate Techniques to Calm Anxiety

1. **Practice Deep Breathing**: Use techniques like 4-7-8 breathing – inhale for 4 seconds, hold for 7, and exhale for 8. It calms your nervous system.
2. **Ground Yourself with the 5-4-3-2-1 Technique**: Identify 5 things you can see, 4 you can touch, 3 you can hear, 2 you can smell, and 1 you can taste to focus on the present moment.
3. **Use Progressive Muscle Relaxation (PMR)**: Tense and then slowly release each muscle group to reduce physical tension.
4. **Carry a Calming Object**: A stress ball, smooth stone, or even a grounding affirmation card can help when anxiety strikes.

Daily Habits to Build Resilience

1. **Establish a Routine**: A consistent daily schedule reduces uncertainty and helps

create a sense of control.

2. **Get Regular Exercise**: Activities like yoga, walking, or cardio release endorphins and reduce stress hormones.
3. **Limit Caffeine and Sugar**: These can heighten anxiety symptoms, so opt for water or herbal teas instead.
4. **Practice Gratitude**: Writing down 3 things you're grateful for daily can shift focus from worries to positive aspects of life.

Mindset and Mental Strategies

1. **Challenge Negative Thoughts**: Identify and reframe anxious thoughts with more realistic, balanced perspectives.
2. **Focus on What You Can Control**: Let go of the uncontrollable and channel your energy into actionable steps.
3. **Break Tasks into Small Steps**: Feeling overwhelmed can lead to anxiety. Tackle challenges one step at a time.

Relaxation and Mindfulness Practices

1. **Try Meditation or Mindfulness**: Apps

like Calm or Headspace guide you in staying present and reducing anxious thoughts.

2. **Use Aromatherapy**: Scents like lavender, chamomile, or eucalyptus can have a calming effect.

Social and Professional Support

1. **Talk to Someone**: Sharing your worries with a trusted friend, family member, or therapist can ease the burden.
2. **Consider Professional Help**: Cognitive-behavioural therapy (CBT) or other therapies can help manage persistent anxiety effectively.

Here are 15 tips to help you build strong mental resilience:

Mindset and Perspective

1. **Adopt a Growth Mindset**: See challenges as opportunities to learn and grow, rather than insurmountable obstacles.
2. **Focus on What You Can Control**: Redirect energy toward what you can influence, instead of worrying about what's beyond your control.
3. **Embrace Change**: Accept that change is inevitable and learn to adapt by staying flexible and open-minded.
4. **Develop Self-Awareness**: Reflect on your thoughts, emotions, and behaviours to understand how they affect your responses.

Habits and Daily Practices

1. **Cultivate Gratitude**: A daily practice of gratitude helps shift focus from stressors to positives in your life.
2. **Set Realistic Goals**: Break larger goals into achievable steps to build momentum

and confidence.

3. **Create a Routine**: A structured daily schedule can bring stability, especially during uncertain times.

Stress Management

1. **Practice Mindfulness or Meditation**: Stay present to reduce stress and build emotional balance.
2. **Learn to Let Go**: Release grudges, regrets, or perfectionism that weigh you down emotionally.
3. **Take Breaks**: Avoid burnout by setting aside time to recharge through rest or leisure activities.

Social and Emotional Support

1. **Build a Strong Support Network**: Surround yourself with people who uplift and encourage you during tough times.
2. **Communicate Effectively**: Express your feelings and ask for help when you need it.

Health and Physical Well-Being

1. **Exercise Regularly**: Physical activity improves both mental clarity and emotional resilience.
2. **Sleep Well**: Quality sleep is essential for emotional regulation and problem-solving.
3. **Practice Self-Care**: Engage in activities that nurture your mind, body, and spirit, such as hobbies or relaxation techniques.

Here are 15 highly effective tips for motivating your team at work:

Create a Positive Work Environment

1. **Set Clear Goals**: Ensure everyone knows the team's mission, goals, and their individual roles in achieving them.
2. **Foster Open Communication**: Encourage feedback, questions, and ideas. Employees feel valued when their voices are heard.
3. **Promote a Culture of Respect**: Recognise each team member's unique contributions and treat everyone with fairness.

Recognise and Reward Efforts

1. **Celebrate Successes**: Acknowledge both big wins and small accomplishments with praise or public recognition.
2. **Provide Incentives**: Offer meaningful rewards, such as bonuses, extra time off, or team outings, for achieving targets.
3. **Personalised Appreciation**: Tailor recognition to each individual's

preferences, such as private praise or a handwritten note.

Empower and Engage

1. **Delegate Authority**: Trust your team with responsibilities and allow them to take ownership of their work.
2. **Involve Them in Decision-Making**: Let team members contribute ideas and solutions to foster a sense of investment.
3. **Provide Opportunities for Growth**: Offer training, mentorship, or new challenges to help them develop professionally.

Build Team Cohesion

1. **Encourage Collaboration**: Create opportunities for teamwork and cross-functional projects to build camaraderie.
2. **Organise Team-Building Activities**: Host activities that are fun and strengthen relationships, such as outings or workshops.

Be an Inspiring Leader

1. **Lead by Example**: Model the work ethic,

attitude, and commitment you want to see in your team.

2. **Provide Regular Feedback**: Offer constructive and timely feedback to help them improve and stay motivated.

Improve Work-Life Balance

1. **Be Flexible**: Accommodate flexible working hours or remote work options where possible.
2. **Encourage Breaks**: Support a healthy balance between work and rest to prevent burnout and maintain enthusiasm.

Here are 15 actionable tips to improve your delegation skills at work:

Mindset and Preparation

1. **Recognise the Value of Delegation**: Understand that delegating tasks is essential for efficiency, team development, and business growth.
2. **Let Go of Perfectionism**: Trust that others can do the work well, even if it's not exactly how you'd do it.
3. **Know Your Team's Strengths**: Assess individual skills, interests, and workloads to delegate tasks effectively.

Choosing What to Delegate

1. **Focus on High-Value Tasks**: Delegate routine or time-consuming tasks so you can focus on strategic priorities.
2. **Delegate for Development**: Assign tasks that will help team members learn new skills or grow professionally.
3. **Avoid Overloading One Person**: Distribute tasks evenly to avoid burnout or resentment.

How to Delegate Effectively

1. **Be Clear About Expectations**: Explain the task's purpose, desired outcomes, deadlines, and quality standards.
2. **Provide Necessary Resources**: Ensure your team has the tools, training, and support needed to succeed.
3. **Set Milestones**: Break the task into smaller steps and agree on check-in points to monitor progress.

Building Trust and Accountability

1. **Trust, Don't Micromanage**: Allow autonomy while staying available for guidance or questions.
2. **Hold People Accountable**: Clearly define who is responsible for what and follow up to ensure accountability.
3. **Be Open to Feedback**: Create an environment where team members feel comfortable asking for help or suggesting improvements.

After Delegation

1. **Provide Constructive Feedback**: Offer

praise for successes and advice for improvement to foster growth.

2. **Learn from Outcomes**: Reflect on what went well and what could be improved to refine your delegation approach.
3. **Acknowledge Their Efforts**: Show appreciation for the work completed to build morale and encourage future collaboration.

Here are 15 essential tips for building and showing empathy:

Developing Empathy

1. **Practice Active Listening**: Give your full attention, avoid interrupting, and validate the speaker's feelings.
2. **Ask Open-Ended Questions**: Encourage others to share their thoughts and feelings by asking questions like, "How did that make you feel?"
3. **Observe Nonverbal Cues**: Pay attention to body language, tone of voice, and facial expressions for deeper understanding.
4. **Expand Your Perspective**: Actively seek to understand viewpoints and experiences different from your own.
5. **Read Fiction**: Stories help you step into someone else's shoes and experience their emotions.

Showing Empathy in Conversations

1. **Validate Emotions**: Acknowledge others' feelings by saying, "That sounds really tough," or "I can see why you'd feel that

way."

2. **Avoid Judging**: Listen without criticism or imposing your own opinions, allowing the person to feel safe sharing.
3. **Share Relatable Experiences**: When appropriate, offer your own experiences to show understanding, but avoid shifting focus to yourself.
4. **Paraphrase and Reflect**: Repeat what the other person says to confirm your understanding and show you're truly listening.

Actions That Demonstrate Empathy

1. **Be Present**: Put away distractions like phones or laptops when someone is sharing something important.
2. **Offer Support**: Ask how you can help or provide small acts of kindness to ease their burden.
3. **Respect Boundaries**: Empathy doesn't mean overstepping; respect their space and preferences.

Empathy as a Habit

1. **Practice Self-Awareness**: Reflect on how your actions and words affect others in building emotional intelligence.
2. **Seek Feedback**: Ask others how they feel about your level of empathy and use their insights to improve.
3. **Engage in Service**: Volunteer or participate in activities that connect you with people in different life circumstances.

Here are 15 tips to help you understand someone's body language effectively:

Face and Eyes

1. **Pay Attention to Eye Contact**:
- Consistent eye contact suggests confidence and engagement.
- Avoidance may indicate discomfort, nervousness, or dishonesty.

2. **Watch Eyebrow Movements**:
- Raised eyebrows can signal surprise, curiosity, or doubt.
- Furrowed brows may indicate confusion or concern.

3. **Notice Facial Expressions**:
- Smiles, frowns, or neutral expressions often reveal emotional states.

Posture

1. **Assess Their Stance**:
- An open posture (e.g., facing you directly, relaxed shoulders) shows receptiveness.
- A closed posture (e.g., crossed arms, leaning away) may indicate defensiveness or disinterest.

2. **Look for Mirroring**:
- When someone subconsciously mirrors your posture or gestures, it signals rapport and connection.

Hands and Arms

1. **Observe Hand Movements**:
- Frequent fidgeting or tapping might indicate nervousness or impatience.
- Open palms suggest honesty and openness, while clenched fists may indicate tension.

2. **Check for Crossed Arms**:
- Crossed arms often signal defensiveness, but context matters—it could also mean the person is cold or comfortable.

Legs and Feet

1. **Notice Leg Positioning**:
- Crossed legs can indicate a closed-off attitude, while uncrossed legs may suggest openness.

2. **Pay Attention to Foot Direction**:
- Feet pointing toward you usually signals

interest while pointing away might suggest a desire to disengage.

Gestures and Movements

1. **Spot Nervous Habits**:
- Biting nails, touching the face, or excessive blinking can indicate anxiety or discomfort.
2. **Interpret Subtle Gestures**:
- Touching the neck or throat may signal insecurity while scratching the head can indicate confusion.

Tone and Pace

1. **Watch Movement Speed**:
- Quick, jerky motions may indicate stress or impatience, while slow, deliberate movements suggest calmness.

Context Matters

1. **Consider the Situation**:
- The meaning of body language often depends on context—nervousness at a job interview differs from nervousness at a party.

2. **Don't Overinterpret**:

- One gesture doesn't tell the whole story. Look for clusters of signals to understand their emotional state.

Empathy and Observation

1. **Match Verbal and Nonverbal Cues**:

- Check if their body language aligns with what they're saying. Incongruence may indicate they're hiding something or feeling conflicted.

Here are 15 top tips for successful business negotiation:

1. Prepare Thoroughly

- Research the other party's needs, objectives, and constraints.
- Know your goals, bottom line, and potential trade-offs.
- Anticipate objections and prepare responses.

2. Establish Clear Objectives

- Define what success looks like for you.
- Identify both your non-negotiables and areas where you can be flexible.

3. Build Rapport

- Start with small talk to establish a connection.
- Building trust early can set a positive tone for the negotiation.

4. Listen Actively

- Focus on understanding the other party's needs and concerns.

- Ask open-ended questions to gather information and clarify intentions.

5. Understand the Other Party's Position

- Learn their goals, pressures, and potential constraints.
- Empathy can help you find common ground and craft solutions.

6. Aim for a Win-Win Outcome

- Look for solutions that provide mutual benefits.
- Avoid viewing negotiation as a zero-sum game where one side wins, and the other loses.

7. Use Silence as a Tool

- After making a point or an offer, pause and allow the other party to respond.
- Silence can create pressure for the other side to fill the gap with concessions or insights.

8. Be Ready to Walk Away

- Know your BATNA (Best Alternative to a

Negotiated Agreement).

- Walking away can sometimes lead to better offers or opportunities elsewhere.

9. Stay Calm and Professional

- Don't let emotions dictate your responses.
- Stay focused on the issues, not personalities.

10. Use Anchoring Wisely

- If you're the first to make an offer, anchor it strategically to set the tone for the discussion.
- Be prepared to adjust based on feedback.

11. Negotiate the Process

- Agree on ground rules for the negotiation upfront.
- This includes setting agendas, timeframes, and decision-making authority.

12. Avoid Common Pitfalls

- Don't overcommit too soon or concede too quickly.

- Avoid making vague agreements that lack clarity or enforceability.

13. Know When to Push and When to Pause

- Recognise when to press for more and when to step back to let the other party process.
- Timing can be just as important as the content of your offer.

14. Document Agreements

- Summarise key points during or immediately after the negotiation.
- Ensure that agreements are clear, documented, and understood by both parties.

15. Follow Up and Build Long-Term Relationships

- After the deal, ensure all terms are implemented as agreed.
- Foster ongoing goodwill for future opportunities by demonstrating reliability and fairness.

Learn From Every Negotiation

- After each negotiation, reflect on what worked, what didn't, and what you can improve.
- Continuous learning will sharpen your skills over time.

Master these tips, and you'll be well-prepared to navigate any business negotiation effectively!

www.ingramcontent.com/pod-product-compliance
Lightning Source LLC
LaVergne TN
LVHW100248210926
848480LV00003B/856

* 9 7 9 8 2 3 1 9 0 4 3 6 5 *